The role of the adult in early years settings

The role of the adult in early years settings

Janet Rose and Sue Rogers

Open University Press

Open University Press
McGraw-Hill Education
McGraw-Hill House
Shoppenhangers Road
Maidenhead
Berkshire
England
SL6 2QL

2021 004 851

email: enquiries@openup.co.uk
world wide web: www.openup.co.uk

and Two Penn Plaza, New York, NY 10121-2289, USA

First published 2012

A catalogue record of this book is available from the British Library

ISBN-13: 978-0-33-524230-6 (pb)
ISBN-10: 0-33-524230-8 (pb)
eISBN: 978-0-33-524231-3

Library of Congress Cataloging-in-Publication Data
CIP data applied for

Typesetting and e-book compilations by
RefineCatch Limited, Bungay, Suffolk
Printed and bound by CPI Group (UK) Ltd, Croydon, CR0 4YY

Fictitious names of companies, products, people, characters and/or data that may be used
herein (in case studies or in examples) are not intended to represent any real individual,
company, product or event.

The **McGraw·Hill** Companies

Contents

Acknowledgements

We would like to thank all the students, practitioners, and colleagues for their contributions to this book and all the children whose stories we tell in our case studies. In addition, we would like to thank Louise Gilbert, Martine Duggan, and Emma Bowery for their helpful comments during the writing of this book. We would also like to extend our thanks to Fiona Richman and Laura Givans of the Open University Press for their guidance and support.

1 Introduction

If you work at the parts, the whole will be a success.

(Anon.)

In this book, we explore the many different ways in which adults interact with young children in early years settings. We introduce the concept of the *plural practitioner*, which acknowledges that the role of the adult in early years settings is complex and demands many different responsibilities, fulfilment of many different tasks, and being many different 'selves'. In a typical day, an early years practitioner may comfort a crying infant, listen to a child talking about their weekend, make pretend cups of tea in the home corner, observe a child's use of the outdoor area, help a child collect resources to make a den, assess a child's communication skills, and complete a child's record of progress. In undertaking these different responsibilities and activities, the practitioner will have been a different 'self' or a combination of different 'selves' depending on what the responsibility or activity entailed.

The notion of 'self' as a physical, psychological, and philosophical concept has been a central idea in western thought for centuries, acknowledging that there are many different dimensions to the self. We all have a 'sense of self' and the way in which we think about ourselves is not limited to one self – we have multiple selves that incorporate different roles, attributes, and behaviours and these vary depending on circumstances. Some of our selves might include 'mother', 'friend', 'partner', and 'colleague', and how we interact, what we do, and how we behave varies from one self to the other. Yet they are all part of the whole self and many of the attributes and behaviours overlap. The same is true of our adult role in our work with young children. In this sense, we are many different selves – we are *plural practitioners*.

The plural practitioner – the seven selves

The *plural practitioner* is a notion that we have applied to reflect the different 'selves' that make up the adult role. It thus recognizes the multiple perspectives of the self in early years practitioners' work with young children. The most helpful way to envisage the 'plural practitioner' concept is to relate the seven selves to the seven colours of the rainbow. Rainbows are formed by the refraction and internal reflection of light inside raindrops, which causes white sunlight to be separated into the colours of the rainbow. The colours of the rainbow are in fact a continuous spectrum of colours rather than a discrete set, but seven colours are distinctive enough to have been named.

This book identifies seven distinctive dimensions of the adult role. The seven selves that constitute the plural practitioner have particular characteristics and encompass particular forms of behaviour but, like rainbow colours, each characteristic or self *blends into and helps to create the next*. The seven different dimensions are therefore presented as *integrated and interactive*. Each forms part of the whole and each contributes to the other (see Figure 1.1).

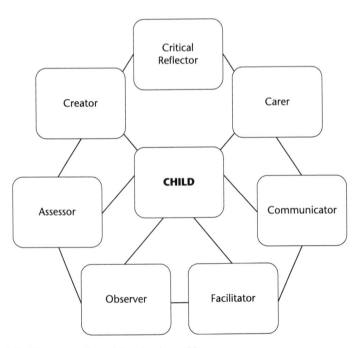

Figure 1.1 The seven selves of the plural practitioner

The seven selves are as follows (and are denoted with a capital letter throughout the book):

- The Critical Reflector
- The Carer
- The Communicator
- The Facilitator
- The Observer
- The Assessor
- The Creator.

Rather than offering a chapter on observation or leadership to guide prospective and existing early years practitioners, we believe that early years practitioners need to view their role in terms of *who they are* rather that simply what they do. The different dimensions of the adult role can be understood as a *process of being* and not just doing, so that the adult role becomes a *dynamic sense of self*.

A rationale for the plural practitioner and the seven selves

Policies relating to early years education and care have a high political profile internationally. In England, recent government initiatives have included creating a graduate early years profession and raising the minimum level of qualifications to generate quality provision. This has drawn attention to the adult role in young children's learning and development, as has recent research. A trawl of the literature shows that many early years texts incorporate some discussion of the adult role. Drawing on this literature, the plural practitioner framework is embedded in theory and research related to early years provision and young children's learning and development. Practitioners' views on their adult role were also sought to supplement the theory and research. Experienced practitioners on early years further training and degree courses based at the authors' institutions were invited during seminar discussions to list key elements of the adult role. These views were drawn upon by the authors in the development of the various characteristics of the plural practitioner.

The notion of the plural practitioner came about as a result of many comments by student practitioners that they had to be a different person depending on what they were doing at any one time. Subsequent discussions moderated by the authors on 'sense of self' and having 'different selves' appeared to resonate with these practitioners. Some of them commented on how what they do links directly to who they are – to their sense of self. Once we had constructed the framework, these practitioners were consulted on how well the 'seven selves' reflected their experiences as adults in early years settings. Their affirmation of these 'seven selves' provided a spur to write this book.

We also took into consideration the curriculum framework for early years provision in England – the Early Years Foundation Stage (EYFS) and the Early Years Professional Status (EYPS) and Qualified Teacher Status (QTS) Standards in England. The EYFS sees two main roles for practitioners, as 'planner' and 'observer'. The EYFS makes it clear that adults have a proactive and deliberate role in generating quality provision for young children. Indeed, government policy for England states that the most important contribution to high-quality provision is 'the quality of the workforce' (DfES, 2007) – in other words, the adults who work with young children. This idea is also supported by research. For example, evidence shows that the key factor for ensuring quality is the adult role (Bertram and Owens, 2007).

Ensuring quality through socially just and child-centred practices

Throughout this book, we argue that the plural practitioner can engender quality early years provision by implementing *child-centred* and *socially just practices*. These are twin agendas upon which early years practitioners can base their role and around which they can build effective provision.

Socially just practices

Socially just practices are about creating *just provision* for children. Different interpretations exist about what socially just practices should look like, but the most common view is that they relate to the establishment of *human rights and equality*. Knowles (2009: 5) describes social justice as 'the principle by which everyone in society should have the opportunity to maximize their life-chances, achieve well-being and flourish'. It is about creating an egalitarian provision in which all participants feel included and valued and are treated with dignity regardless of their abilities, ethnicity, social class or gender.

The importance of having socially just provision is borne out by evidence that shows how issues such as ethnicity, social class, and gender can have a direct impact on children's educational outcomes (Alexander, 2010). For example, children's socio-economic status can predict their literacy performance in school. We know that children from lower socio-economic groups (disadvantaged backgrounds) frequently do less well than those from higher socio-economic groups (advantaged backgrounds). How factors such as social class, ethnic group, and gender affect children's progress is a complex issue, but the important point to remember is the potential impact these factors have on the child, particularly in the early years. One study, for instance, has shown how children from an early age are aware of the limitations placed on them by their low social status and household income (Hirsch, 2007), and other research has demonstrated that young children can internalize messages about power and privilege related to ideas around gender, race or fairness and this can be reflected in their play (Hyland, 2010). For example, children practise the skills necessary for good citizenship during their socio-dramatic play as they negotiate roles and responsibilities (MacNaughton and Williams, 2004), and work by Siraj-Blatchford (1994) shows that the foundations for justice and equality are laid in the early years. The Effective Provision of Preschool Education (EPPE) project (Sylva et al., 2010) has also highlighted how quality preschool provision can help to combat social exclusion. Two recent governmental reports have drawn on such evidence to emphasize the important role that early years professionals can play in helping to counteract some of the effects of disadvantage and so narrow the socio-economic gaps in society and improve children's life-chances (Field, 2010; Allen, 2011).

In England, it is a statutory requirement for early years practitioners to be 'alert to the early signs of needs that could lead to later difficulties and [respond] quickly and appropriately, involving other agencies as necessary' (DfES, 2007: 1.14). The EYFS states several prerequisites regarding early years practitioners' responsibilities towards ensuring equal opportunities, such as fostering 'positive attitudes to diversity and difference – not only so that every child is included and not disadvantaged, but also so that they learn from the earliest age to value diversity in others and grow up making a positive contribution to society' (DfES, 2007: 1.14). This means that practitioners need to remove or help to overcome 'barriers for children' where they already exist and provide opportunities for all children to experience a 'challenging and enjoyable programme of learning and development' regardless of their 'ethnicity, culture or religion, home language, family background, learning difficulties or disabilities, gender or ability' (DfES, 2007: 1.15).

Child-centred practices

Like social justice, the concept of child-centred education has many definitions and interpretations and is both revered and contested in equal measure in the literature. The concept of child-centred education is commonly traced to the philosophers Rousseau and Dewey, with *child-centred pedagogy* employed by pioneers such as Froebel and Isaacs since the beginning of the twentieth century. It was championed in England by the Plowden Report (Central Advisory Council for Education, 1967), which heralded a child-centred approach to teaching practices (although the extent to which this occurred in practice is a matter of some debate). The report was based on a view of the child as active, exploratory, curious, creative, playful, and sociable. One of its claims was that 'children should be allowed to be themselves' and declared 'at the heart of the educational process lies the child' (Central Advisory Council for Education, 1967). The EYFS reflects many of the attributes associated with child-centred provision. These include viewing the child as intrinsically curious and capable, respecting children's rights as well as their needs and interests, and a commitment to active learning and free play. Child-centred practices envisage children as curious knowledge seekers who actively contribute to their own development, and see them as active agents in their own learning.

A key approach to following a child-centred pedagogy is the adoption of what is known as 'developmentally appropriate practice'. This notion was developed in the USA by organizations such as the National Association for the Education of Young Children (NAEYC, 2008) and in England by academics such as Blenkin and Kelly (1988). It refers to the kind of 'educare' practices that are considered to be most appropriate for young children. The ideas behind developmentally appropriate practice are based on research into the most effective ways to optimize young children's learning and development. The essential principles behind developmentally appropriate practice include active learning experiences, multi-sensory approaches, and pretend play (Goswami and Bryant, 2007). A longitudinal, cross-cultural study on preschool experiences in ten different countries found that developmentally appropriate practice works best for younger children (Montie et al., 2007).

The concept of a developmentally appropriate practice has been extended and revised to take into account cultural diversity and to acknowledge that not all child development theory reflects sufficiently the contextualized nature of learning and development. Although most child development theory is still based upon predominantly westernized views of knowing the child and understanding childhood activity, it is now commonly accepted that child development is not simply a matter of individual cognition but 'a process of growing into a culture' (Walsh, 2005). This more contemporary perspective of young children's development and learning has reconceptualized developmentally appropriate practice as 'contextually appropriate practice', in which the context, the individual child, and the interactions between them all play their part (see, for example, Fleer, 2005). At the heart of contemporary child-centred practice lie relationships with others. For example, Dahlberg and Moss (2005) note that we exist through our relationships with others bound within a particular socio-cultural context. This view reflects what is known as a *socio-cultural perspective* of human development and learning, and these ideas are explored throughout the book. We recognize that children can actively manage their own contributions as they participate in social engagements and that learning is a process of co-construction. Our use of the term 'child-centred practices', therefore, embraces this broader notion of the individual child operating within socio-cultural relationships and contexts.

The various chapters in this book portray the seven selves in terms of the socially just and child-centred agendas that drive the plural practitioner's practice. But how are we to achieve this in practice? This question leads us to another central theme of this book – the practical ways in which practitioners can ensure that their provision, *particularly through their interactions and engagement with young children*, fulfil the aims of socially just and child-centred provision. This is done by focusing attention on adult–child interactions.

Adult–child interactions

We draw here on some recent research we undertook on practitioners' understanding of the adult role and the dilemmas that they encounter. This research suggests some confusion exists among professionals in relation to what this role should entail, particularly in terms of the appropriate nature and extent of direction, intervention, and interaction with the child. The uncertainly and confusion surrounding adult intervention may arise from apparently conflicting research and theory on this role and possible misinterpretation of the statutory requirements of the EYFS, which supports both adult-led and child-initiated activity. Some of the dilemmas the student practitioners faced included:

- At what point should I intervene?
- What level and kind of support is appropriate?
- When does intervention become interference?
- What kinds of questions are appropriate?
- When do I tell them the right answer or help them?
- Will my intervention stop it from being child-led?
- Does child-led mean the same thing as child-initiated?

The aim of this book, therefore, is to help practitioners to address such questions by illuminating the *nature of the interactions* adults have with young children (and to some extent, other adults) in supporting learning and development and how these might translate into practice. MacNaughton and Williams (2004) cite research that shows how, in a typical day, early years practitioners might have over a thousand 'interpersonal interactions' with children. UNICEF (2001) summed up the implications of the adult role and adult–child interactions: 'Choices made and actions taken . . . during this critical period affect not only how a child develops but also how a country progresses'.

Each of the chapters directly addresses important aspects of practice that maximize socially just and child-centred practices through our interactions with children. In addition, the book will help to clarify the adult role in both *adult-led and child-initiated* activities.

What the EYFS and practitioners say about adult-led and child-initiated activities

The EYFS provides its own explanation of 'child-initiated' and 'adult-led' activities, stating that 'when a child engages in a self chosen pursuit, this is child-initiated activity' (DfES, 2007: 1.19). By contrast, adult-led activities are defined as activities that are selected by adults 'to encourage a particular aspect of learning, or discuss a particular topic': 'As well as leading activities and encouraging child-led activities, you should support and extend all children's development and learning by being an active listener and joining in and intervening when appropriate' (DfES, 2007: 2.7).

At the same time, the Practice Guidance suggests that even in activities first led or initiated by an adult, the activity might become child-initiated. This suggests a child-centred approach in which the adult must take the lead from the child wherever possible. The Practice Guidance endorses practice that enables a child to take 'ownership of an activity' and to allow a child to 'subvert' it 'to a different purpose than intended' (DfES, 2007: 1.19). The interpretation of adult-led activities in the Practice Guidance also acknowledges that in adult-led activities, the 'child's need for adult involvement will decrease over time as they master the skill' (DfES, 2007: 1.20).

How do early years practitioners translate these requirements and guidance? Recent research undertaken by the authors reveals some mixed interpretations of the adult role in early years settings. One hundred experienced early years practitioners who were undertaking Early Years Practitioner Status (EYPS), a newly introduced early years qualification in England, were asked to describe what they understood by the terms 'child-initiated' and 'adult-led' activities. The research revealed a range of interpretations, but the majority of practitioners held a polarized 'either/or' view in relation to adult-led and child-initiated activities. For one practitioner, 'adult-led' meant that 'the adult sets the agenda, rules, and aims of the activity and tells the child when and where the play can happen, while child-initiated means that the child chooses what, how, when, and where to play'. Most practitioners in the study also considered that in adult-led activities, control was always retained by the adult so as to meet particular learning objectives or desired outcomes. Often adult-led activities were associated with terms such as 'closed' or 'structured', while child-initiated activities were associated with terms such as 'open-ended' or 'free'. The interpretation of the two types of activities appears to centre on issues of control and whether this lies with the adult or the child. There were also some mixed interpretations of what the adult role ought to be. Some practitioners felt that child-initiated activities should never involve an adult, while others considered that it was appropriate for the adult to support the child in child-initiated activities or to intervene to promote particular skills, knowledge, and/or understanding. In other cases, the adult role was viewed as a 'guide', 'support', 'prompt' or 'scaffold' for both adult-led and child-initiated activities. A few practitioners envisaged a more direct teaching role, where the adult 'dictates', 'directs' or 'determines' what happens, although this style of interaction was always associated with adult-led activities. Some also considered that only adult-led play had a deliberate educational intention, while others felt that child-initiated play always entailed learning on the part of the child.

This research resonates with other perspectives in the field regarding the degree of adult involvement in young children's learning. As we mentioned earlier, research (Bennett et al., 1997; Rose, 2001; Maynard and Chicken, 2010) has demonstrated that a common tension experienced by early years practitioners is whether to 'intervene' and that different pedagogical approaches within children's play entail both subtle and stark contrasts in terms of the amount or type of adult interaction and involvement in children's activities (Miller and Pound, 2011). Exploration of other literature confirms the confusing parameters of the adult role presented. For example, Bruce's work on 'free flow play' could be read as non-interventionist, as do some interpretations of the work of Piaget. Similarly, Goldschmeid's notion of 'heuristic play' presents the adult as a 'silent companion' who sits near the young child while he or she freely explores the various resources provided by the adult. In contrast, the work of Vygotsky and Bruner supports a more interactive stance in which the adult actively 'scaffolds' the child's learning and can act as a primary vehicle for knowledge construction, while Bandura's social learning theory emphasizes the importance of adult role-modelling for children, suggesting a clear proactive stance.

How are practitioners to accommodate seemingly contradictory advice, especially when coming from such esteemed theorists? Alexander (2010: 95) sums up the main essence of the debate regarding the adult role by asking whether practitioners ought to 'develop a child or watch a child develop'. Here, we provide the framework for helping early years practitioners to forge a robust understanding of a range of theories and to relate these to the different selves of their adult role. Our aim is to offer practitioners the opportunity to develop a clear sense of self in their practice and so help them to clarify their role in children's learning and in developing high-quality early years practice around the notions of *child-centred* and *socially just practices*. In doing so, this book uses the terms 'child-initiated' and 'adult-initiated' activities in place of terms such as 'child-led' and 'adult-directed'. We consider that the use of the terms *child-initiated* and *adult-initiated activities* can help practitioners to better understand the reciprocal nature of adult–child interactions and might help to diminish uncertainties regarding adult intervention. By viewing all activities and exchanges as a process of initiation that immediately becomes an interconnected negotiation, rather than as an act of being led or directed by either the child or the adult, we can envisage the adult–child relationship as one that involves interchangeable processes of 'give-and-take' and mutual co-construction. These ideas will be explored throughout the book.

Outline of the book

Chapter 1 introduces the Critical Reflector self and highlights the importance of creating critical reflective practice to ensure socially just and child-centred practices. To achieve these aims, it is necessary to challenge existing assumptions and expectations about our values, practice, and constructions of the child. The chapter emphasizes the need to develop communities of practitioners who contribute to a learning organization and the establishment of evidence-informed practice through a research 'mindset' and an ongoing evaluation of provision.

Chapter 2 focuses on the Carer self, which is framed within a perspective of an 'ethic of care' that we argue ought to underpin all practitioners' work with young children. This ethic of care addresses the role of the early years practitioner in laying the foundations for social justice. The chapter shows how practising an inclusive approach within their practice, by engendering a sense of belonging and attachment and by supporting the development of emotional intelligence in the child, socially just and child-centred practices can be realized by the Carer self.

Chapter 3 addresses the Communicator self and the most effective ways of communicating meaning and developing understanding with children. It embraces the understanding that communication and social interaction are intrinsic to learning and development. It draws attention to the various processes involved in communicating with young children and how these might translate into practice. In doing so, it offers a framework by which practitioners can ensure more socially just and child-centred practices by tuning into the child's needs and interests.

Chapter 4 focuses on the Facilitator self, which is viewed in terms of enabling, engaging, and mediating. It emphasizes the reciprocal and responsive relationship between adult and child in easing children's progress. In particular, it interrogates the adult's role in terms of empowering young children, promoting their autonomy, decision-making, and problem-solving – all hallmarks of child-centred practices. At the same time, it explores the adult role in scaffolding and supporting learning and development, helping children to create connections and make sense of the world. Particular attention is given to the notion of sustained shared thinking in this process.

Chapter 5 explores the Observer self and its place in young children's learning and development. It introduces the Observation, Assessment, Planning (OAP) cycle, which is an intrinsic part of early years practice, and establishes its meaning and purpose. The chapter clarifies the part played by the Observer self in understanding and knowing the children in its care, which can help practitioners to establish a socially just and child-centred approach to their practice. Particular attention is paid to the process of how children make sense of their worlds.

Chapter 6 moves onto the next stage of the OAP cycle and evaluates the Assessor self. It clarifies the process of analysing observations and how these relate to more formalized assessment frameworks such as the Foundation Stage Profile. Attention is drawn to how our analysis of children's progress is affected by how we view children, and the various influences that affect children's learning and development are acknowledged. The chapter also explores the power dimensions of assessment and their implications for issues related to social justice. It also considers possibilities for supporting children's self-evaluation of their learning, reflecting a child-centred mode of assessment.

Chapter 7 brings us to the last part of the OAP cycle – the Creator self. This term has been deliberately chosen in place of the term 'planner' to emphasize the creative dimensions of the adult role and the need to create a contextually and developmentally appropriate learning environment for young children. The chapter highlights the planned, received, and hidden curriculum that young children will encounter, since this will help to determine whether the curriculum reflects socially just principles, as well as the importance of creating multi-sensory, embedded, imaginative, and explorative experiences that cater for diverse needs and interests. The role of play and its place in sowing the seeds of child-centred practices is highlighted.

The book does not encompass all the key aspects of practice that early years practitioners are likely to come across in their work with young children, or the range of challenges and constraints they might face. Nor have we attended to other significant dimensions of the adult role, such as inter-agency working and professional collaboration, leadership and team working, and the particular issues related to working with children with additional needs. This was a deliberate decision to allow us to focus on key attributes of the adult role with a particular emphasis on the nature of interactions with young children, which we consider incorporates a *minimal entitlement* for all children. We do not address special circumstances or additional input that might be necessary for children with particular needs but we do offer a way of envisaging our role in working with young children no matter what their circumstances, in the spirit of propagating socially just and child-centred practices. In this respect, the book highlights the significance of the adult role in helping to counteract some of the potential barriers to children's progress and well-being.

To support the rationale behind the seven selves, we provide some under-pinning theory on how and why young children's development and learning occurs that is pertinent to early years practitioners fulfilling their adult role. We acknowledge that the research and theory drawn upon relies heavily on western perspectives of child development and learning and therefore may not take sufficient consideration of cross-cultural dimensions. Connections are made within each chapter to different pedagogical and ideological approaches to early years education from around the world to tease out those elements that reflect child-centred and socially just practices, as well as to acknowledge the influence of such pedagogical approaches in early years settings in the UK.

The following chapters portray the interconnected seven selves of the plural practitioner which reflect the essence of the adult role, and we hope will help early years practitioners to see that *who they are* and *what they do* are indivisible.

2   The Critical Reflector

Reflective thinking turns experience into insight.

(John C. Maxwell)

We begin our exploration of the different selves of the adult role with the Critical Reflector and we hope that by placing it first, we communicate its significance. The chapter draws attention to the way in which practitioners' values, beliefs, attitudes, knowledge, and assumptions about young children directly affect the provision they seek to create and the nature of their interactions with children. It reviews what being a Critical Reflector entails and clarifies what is meant by the term 'critical reflector'. It is shown that practitioners need to systematically examine their thinking and actions through critically reflective research on practice. Such an examination includes the need by practitioners to engage continuously with their understanding of their professional knowledge and its application as well as ensuring that their personal construction of what children mean to them and how they envisage child-centred practices are robustly formulated and grounded in egalitarian principles. It is suggested that practitioners adopt 'action research' as a method for reviewing the quality of their practice and daily interactions with children. The chapter shows how undertaking action research can help early years practitioners to develop a 'learning community' in which all adults and children can flourish. Underlying the Critical Reflector dimension to the adult role is the need to ensure the kind of child-centred and socially just practices that lie at the core of this book.

The critically reflective professional

Statutory obligations

The idea of being a reflective practitioner is a well-established phenomenon. The Early Years Professional Status (EYPS) Standards (CWDC, 2007) require practitioners to '[r]eflect on and evaluate the impact of practice, modifying approaches where necessary' (S38) and '[t]o take a creative and constructively critical approach towards innovation and adapt practice' (S39). The Qualified Teacher Status Standards contain similar phrases that require teachers to reflect on and adapt their practice and adopt a critical stance towards changing practice (Q7 and Q8). The Critical Reflector dimension of the adult role acknowledges the requirements for early years professionals to be reflective practitioners and to evaluate and improve provision, but what does this actually mean in practice?

The notion of critically reflective thinking

One definition of reflective thinking for an early years practitioner is the ability to think back on an activity that has occurred or a situation that exists within the setting, ponder on its success or failure, and make some kind of evaluation to help improve the quality of provision. This could literally be about anything – an existing policy, an exchange with a parent, an adult-initiated activity, a conversation with a child. For the Critical Reflector, however, reflective thinking entails much more than mere contemplation – there is an assumption that such reflection will take on a more *critical* orientation. So what makes reflective thinking more critical? Many different forms and levels of reflective thinking have been identified, and most of the debates about reflective thinking revolve around distinguishing between more superficial types or levels of thinking and a deeper, more probing approach. These are often described as being 'technical' or 'critical' in nature (Gore, 1987).

A *technical reflector* thinks in terms of goal achievement and practical issues. For example, he or she will think back on an activity and thoughtfully consider whether the goals of that activity have been met, whether the child has achieved the standard required, and whether there were sufficient resources for task completion – the pre-specified goal becomes the main focus for reflection. In contrast, a *critical reflector* will have a different agenda and will be more concerned about two other key aspects regarding the activity – whether the child's needs and interests have been accommodated, and whether the activity ensured socially just practices. The Critical Reflector ensures the reflective process is personal and meets the child's needs and interests – what is termed *child-centred practice* – as well as thinking more broadly about ensuring the provision is inclusive and anti-discriminatory – what is termed *socially just practice*.

Technical and critical reflection

Although we have distinguished between two types of reflector here, it is important not to view a technical reflector and a critical reflector in 'either/or' terms. *Both kinds of reflection* are necessary to evaluate effectively the aspect of practice being reviewed. Indeed, viewing reflection as always incorporating immediate, pragmatic aims as well as deeper interests in a spectrum of increasingly sophisticated thinking is a more helpful approach. Practitioners need to appraise more perfunctory practicalities such as ensuring their practice fulfils the specific learning goals of the Early Years Foundation Stage (EYFS) and other policy requirements, but to be a Critical Reflector, practitioners need to ensure that such aims do not detract from an overriding impetus to scrutinize provision in terms of the twin issues of generating *child-centred* and *socially just practices*.

Critical pedagogy

In the Introduction, we began to explore what socially just practices might entail for the adult role. As a Critical Reflector, it means always checking that the setting's provision and all interactions that occur with others are in accordance with principles of *equality*. This means that the Critical Reflector will help to ensure that the children in his or her care are not exposed to unjust or unfair practices and that tolerance and respect for diversity is promoted. Such an approach has been termed 'critical pedagogy' (Shor, 1992) and calls for practitioners to ensure that they question practices that might inhibit a child's potential or restrict their possibilities for progressing their learning and development.

The implications of the social and economic benefits of early intervention were outlined in the Introduction to this book, which emphasized the adult role in this process. Clearly, it is not possible for early years practitioners to change a child's home circumstances. But they can play a part in improving children's potential by providing opportunities for learning and development during this crucial period, by providing some kind of *buffer* from adversity and by ensuring that all children are treated and perceived equally. Early intervention approaches have direct links to ideas of social justice, but need to be framed within critically reflective practice to ensure that differences in children's culture, gender, ethnicity, and socio-economic background do not inhibit their progress. The early years setting can alleviate these issues and provide 'accessible and equitable care and education' for all children (Craft and Paige-Smith, 2008: 15).

By having a social justice agenda within the critically reflective process, the Critical Reflector helps to ensure that reflection is more robust and takes into account both the direct context and indirect influences that might be affecting the child's learning and development. In Chapter 6, we consider the work of Bronfenbrenner (1979) in helping to understand how early years practitioners can ensure that their reflections on practice consider all the potential influences that might affect the child and inhibit ethical practices. Bronfenbrenner (1979) devised a model of children's development, also known as the ecological systems theory, that is interpreted in terms of the *relationships* between the child and the contexts or *environments* that the child encounters. The environments and relationships exist at different social, cultural, political, and historical levels. For example, the EYFS is a 'political' and 'cultural' influence that directly affects a 'social' influence, namely the early years practitioner, who in turn has a direct bearing on what the child experiences. The child is viewed as an active participant in the relationships and environments. This means that we always need to position our 'work and practices within the complex relationships with children, their families, other services and wider policies' (Craft and Paige-Smith, 2008: 22), as each 'layer' will have a direct or indirect impact on the child.

Schön (1987) has theorized that reflection does not just take place in the aftermath of an action, but also occurs *during* the action. Schön calls this 'reflection on action' and 'reflection in action' respectively, and critical reflection requires both. A more critical style of reflection will therefore not necessarily look for finite answers or solutions but will be interested in deepening self-awareness and understanding of the processes of young children's learning and development in a continuous quest for improved quality of provision. In other words, for the Critical Reflector, enhancing their practice will not just be a matter of resolving problems or finding solutions, they will always view the setting as problematic and in need of questioning.

The ongoing journey of critical reflection

One rationale for envisaging the reflective process as unremitting is the pace at which our world is changing. As practitioners, we need to be conscious of the shifts that are occurring within the various influences identified by Bronfenbrenner such as within families, within society, and on a global scale. In England, such shifts in the early years are reflected in the profound changes that have occurred over the last decade in the professionalization of the workforce (with the introduction of EYPS), state-supported childcare (now eligible for all 3- and 4-year-olds and even some 2-year-olds), and expansion of provision (with the introduction of Sure Start children's centres). Moreover, technological advances, the globalized economy, the changing ecological environment, and history itself show that nothing stays the same. We need to adopt a perspective that is alert to the potential impact of ongoing change and acknowledges that the journey for improving the quality of provision is never ending. This means that our own practice may need to change and thus our professional thinking. Indeed, most of the literature on thinking and knowing purports that the main indicator for sophisticated and higher levels of thinking is the acknowledgement that critical reflection is a 'process of interpreting and reinterpreting, of understanding and re-understanding', in which 'the quest for valid interpretations is a recursive, circular activity' (Unrau, 1997: 22).

Although we may reach conclusions and adopt specific practices that we decide, after critical reflection, make for the best possible course of action under existing circumstances, we do so with the understanding that such practices are always in a *state of transition* – Perry (1981) calls this 'commitment in relativism'. Perry considered that as a Critical Reflector he would always

> be wholehearted while tentative, fight for my values, yet respect others, believe my deepest values right, yet be ready to learn. I see that I shall be retracing this whole journey over and over – but, I hope, more wisely.
>
> (Perry, 1981: 79)

A critical spirit

The Critical Reflector, therefore, is always evolving but to sustain this journey, he or she needs to be imbued with what has been called a 'critical spirit' (Siegel, 1999). This basically is a desire or disposition to think at a critical level – an eagerness, a willingness, a curiosity to improve practice. Such an outlook incorporates an emotional element that helps to motivate the Critical Reflector to examine their practices. The emotional or affective dimension to reflective thinking is now widely recognized and is closely linked to our personal value system, such as what kind of provision we think children should have. We will see in the next chapter how emotional signals can help to focus our attention and lead us into conscious reflection on the *value* of particular activities. Nias (1993) also highlights the 'deeply emotional relationship' practitioners have with their work and how educational practice is 'highly charged with feeling'. She suggests the reasons lie with the nature of the profession, since it involves 'intensive personal interactions' and entails 'close, even intimate, contact with other human beings for whose conduct and progress [practitioners] are held responsible' (Nias, 1993: 296). Early years practitioners need to be passionate about their work and motivated to improve the lives of the children in their care (Dadds, 1995; Edgington, 2005), and a critical spirit helps to spur them into action. In turn, the process of critical reflection can help to generate positive feelings within the practitioner's sense of self and their personal professional identity, which consequently bolsters the practitioner's critical spirit in a cycle of ever increasing positive growth. The positive emotional impact of being a Critical Reflector is shown in Case Study 2.1, which portrays how one practitioner was charged with excitement and felt an empowering liberation by critically reflecting on her practice.

Finally, in addition to continuous critical reflection and being endowed with a critical spirit, the Critical Reflector needs to *take action*. Thought and action operate as a holistic, integrated system (Yinger and Hendricks-Lee, 1993) and so reflection cannot be distinguished from action, since all the actions we take are ultimately derived from what we think. The following sections explore how the Critical Reflector takes such action.

Questioning our professional knowledge

Professional knowledge

One of the key messages of this chapter is how our practical actions are informed by our decision-making and how this decision-making is ultimately driven by our personal system of beliefs, values, knowledge, and attitudes. We have collectively termed this system of beliefs, values, knowledge, and attitudes 'professional knowledge', and it is this professional knowledge that essentially determines the quality of young children's experiences in a particular setting. Our composite professional knowledge is derived from a complex range of sources and contexts, which include formal learning theories, such as Piaget's theory of cognitive development, and Vygotsky's views on the importance of the socio-cultural context in learning. We know that different theoretical views of children's learning and development affect practitioners' educational practices and the kind of qualities of the child that are fostered and valued within each view (Daniels and Shumow, 2003).

Intuitive theories

But professional knowledge is more than child development theory. Professional knowledge also comprises what might be called 'intuitive theories', which are derived from a practitioner's personal views about how children should be treated and supported in their development and learning. These intuitive theories might also be influenced by and expanded upon by experiences in settings and what is picked up from other practitioners. Such intuitive theories have been called 'craft knowledge' or 'practical wisdom' (Elliott, 1993). Professional knowledge also incorporates our understanding of early years settings – what they are, what they are for – and other *paradigmatic perspectives* or 'world views' about early years provision. Such views are likely to have been influenced by government perspectives enshrined in legitimized frameworks, such as the EYFS and the EYPS and QTS Standards in England. These legal frameworks will also contribute to practitioners' formalization of their professional knowledge.

Whatever knowledge practitioners draw upon – grand academic theories, personal beliefs based on their own upbringing or experiences, expertise from other practitioners or legal frameworks and government policies – they all become *personal interpretations*. However well-informed a practitioner might be about quality provision for a child, they will still need to make their own sense of experiences and knowledge acquired and to check that the professional knowledge that guides their decision-making is appropriate and applicable.

Challenging our professional knowledge

Having a good knowledge of child development is considered essential for the early years professional (Alexander, 2010), but practitioners need to *apply* this theory to their practice in meaningful ways. Being a Critical Reflector can help practitioners to do this. In addition, intuitive theories – those that are not derived from training, academic research or theory – also need to be scrutinized to ensure that they do not contain invalid assumptions about young children, particularly when they are based on moral judgements and social expectations that do not benefit all children. This becomes more crucial if practitioners settle into unreflective, habitual practices that are never challenged or questioned.

Our thinking is essentially a *personalized construction of reality*. Whatever the source of such knowledge (child development theory, legal frameworks or personal experiences), the potential for misconstruing reality exists. Mezirow has shown how

> we tend to accept and integrate experiences that comfortably fit our frame of reference and to discount those that do not. Thus, our current frame of reference serves as the boundary condition for interpreting the meaning of an experience.
>
> (Mezirow, 1991: 32)

As we learn from our experiences, there is the potential danger that we might misapprehend or mis-learn from them as we attempt to accommodate new learning into existing constructions and value orientations. Our personal interpretation of reality is therefore potentially fallible.

Socio-cultural forces

At the same time, it is recognized how socio-cultural forces influence an individual's representation of reality. Knowledge acquisition is an interpersonal process and is mediated by social activity in specific contexts (Vygotsky, 1978). We don't just actively construct the world; the form, content, and quality of our cognitive products and processes are heavily influenced by the 'expression and the transmission of cultural norms and practices which become the "stuff" of learning' (Barer-Stein, 1987: 89). We also know that over time, cultural values and beliefs are 'inherited' through inter-generational social interactions that become legitimized in society, a process Gadamer (1989) refers to as 'historical consciousness'. As Edwards (2000: 198) puts it, 'our interpretations as we try to make sense of our worlds are mediated in part by the cultural past reified in the cultural present'. In other words, as we construct our 'model' of the world, we become 'encultured' into particular ways of viewing the world

– these are ideological conventions that are historically constituted (Bruner, 1986, 1990).

Professional enculturation

The same process applies when we enter the realm of professional practice. O'Hanlon (1993: 245) refers to this phenomenon as 'professional enculturation', which involves practitioners acquiring 'prevailing educational trends and philosophies' that are blended into existing personal experiences, needs, and values. When working in an early years setting, we are entering a cultural heritage of early years provision that contains prototypes of how to work with young children – the traditions, habits, and precedents of early years practice. We referred earlier to this cultural heritage as 'craft knowledge'. Another term used is 'folk pedagogy' (Olson and Bruner, 1996). This is combined with our personal biographical heritage, which has been shaped by our own educational experiences and conceptions of the adult role and how it should be enacted – including the perceptions we have acquired during the course of our professional training. As Critical Reflectors, we need to be aware of all these personal and socio-cultural 'forces' that will affect what we do with young children. We need to ensure that these are articulated, particularly if they are uncritically absorbed as 'natural' and 'common sense' practices simply because that is the way things have always been done. The need to challenge prevailing practices that have become popularized and legitimized over time is imperative if such practices misrepresent or marginalize young children. The implication here is that if practitioners do not challenge their professional knowledge sufficiently, they will perpetuate what may be inappropriate and unjust ways of working with young children.

Uprooting hidden assumptions

Critical reflection is seen by many as the means of overcoming the problems of ingrained practice and for uprooting hidden assumptions. Torff (1999: 210) calls for the engagement of reflective thinking to 'encounter and evaluate . . . uncritically held beliefs, and to develop a greater understanding of the limitations and pervasiveness of folk pedagogy'. As Critical Reflectors, we can do this by undertaking a process that Brookfield (1995) calls 'assumption hunting'.

Challenging assumptions and transformations of the self

Assumption hunting

For Brookfield (1987: 1), critical reflection is essentially a process of 'calling into question the assumptions underlying our customary, habitual ways of thinking and acting and then being ready to think and act differently on the basis of this critical questioning'. Thus Brookfield (1995) believes it is the unearthing and scrutiny of various assumptions that ensures reflection becomes critical. *Assumption hunting* includes viewing our practice 'from as many unfamiliar angles as possible' (Brookfield, 1995: 28). These multiple perspectives or 'lenses' help to ensure that the validity and accuracy of assumptions are scrutinized.

Habitual practice

The need to continuously scrutinize our assumptions is borne out by the extensive literature on teacher thinking, which has shown how educational practice tends to become routinized. This research is equally applicable to early years contexts. One of the reasons our practice becomes routinized is because we invariably have to act 'in the moment' and draw on automatic and routine responses (Mitchell and Marland, 1989). If we feel compelled to alter this routine, we tend 'not to critically evaluate the alternatives' and instead we prefer to seek confirmation for the choices made (Shavelson and Stern, 1981: 487). This is partly due to our reliance upon what are known as 'heuristics'. These are 'implicit rules that people are unaware of and use in complex tasks in order to select information, classify objects or persons, or revise their knowledge' (Shavelson and Stern, 1981: 469). A classic example is the 'representativeness heuristic'. This is the way we categorize the children in a setting by comparing the attributes that they might have with the attributes of a particular category or stereotype in our minds. We might encounter a particular boy who behaves in a certain way that matches a presupposition or 'representative heuristic' of a 'typical, naughty boy'. In doing so, we make causal inferences about that child which direct our expectations and behaviour with that child.

Overall, the research literature implies that practitioners need to question their professional knowledge base and expose unreflective, habitual practice. This way, assumptions about children and practices can be reconstituted so that they become more inclusive and integrative in order to fit child-centred and socially just practices. Assumption hunting can create an awareness of how our assumptions influence our thoughts and actions and then 'imagine and explore alternatives to existing ways of thinking and living' (Brookfield, 1987: 8). In turn, this brings about a 'change in the self' (Brookfield, 1995).

Transformational learning

The changes in the self that can be brought about by the process of assumption hunting have been elaborated by Mezirow's (1991) theory of *transformational learning*. This theory helps us to understand what we can do as Critical Reflectors to ensure that our assumptions about what we do in practice with young children are properly challenged and critically reflected upon. Mezirow's theory of critical reflection is encapsulated in his beliefs about our need to transform invalid perspectives that we might have about our practices. He holds that reflection takes on a critical turn when it involves a critique of 'presuppositions' (what he calls 'premise reflection') – these are the assumptions we have about practice and are essentially 'habits of expectation' or 'organised representations of an event that serve as prototypes or norms for what is expected' (Mezirow, 1991: 48). They are like the stereotypical 'representative heuristic' mentioned earlier. They are the theory, beliefs, values, attitudes, and emotional reactions that make up our professional knowledge and 'guide the way in which we experience, feel, understand, judge, and act upon particular situations' (Mezirow, 1991: 48). In this way, they act as a 'perceptual' filter that may distort our interpretations of reality leading to misrepresentations or the perpetuation of unjust practices. This relates to the previous discussion on how our professional knowledge is constructed.

Perspective transformation

Mezirow acknowledges both the personal and socio-cultural influences on the process of professional knowledge construction, and stresses the need to examine our built-in assumptions given the power they have to govern our interpretation of the world. He calls for practitioners to critically reflect on their presuppositions and transform them via the assessment or reassessment of assumptions, a process he calls 'perspective transformation'.

So how do practitioners go about assumption hunting? The following sections reveal a valuable and practical way to help early years practitioners to ensure their practice is critically reflective through the adoption of action research within a learning community and is illustrated using case studies.

Case study 2.1   Assumption hunting and questioning professional knowledge

As a Reception teacher, Sarah was concerned about those children she perceived to be 'reluctant speakers'. She decided to undertake some action research and observe children in different circumstances from those she normally undertook, such as in the role play area. This initiated an 'assumption hunting' process within her thinking. The research served to demonstrate how Sarah's predictions of children's abilities were flawed. She noted how the research had 'made me aware of how easy it is, as a teacher, to underestimate the abilities and competencies of children who are reluctant speakers. It also has encouraged me to broaden my assessments of children's speaking – looking at more informal talk'. The results of

Sarah's observations prompted the uprooting and reorganisation of ingrained assumptions about children's communicative skills and inveterate beliefs about the adult role. This led her to retranslate her overall conception of the adult role, as she realised that 'teachers don't always have to interact with the child for the child to be learning or to be doing something of value. That some constructive play situation, one that they're structuring themselves, is of equal if not greater value than a teacher led activity . . . There's so much more to children's communication than just adult–child talk'. Sarah had always felt that 'intervention [was] something you feel you ought to do . . . I felt pressured as a teacher to intervene and take the language onto a higher level'. Sarah considered that this was 'what was expected' of her and vocalised the sources of this pressure to 'intervene' and 'be doing something' to include 'parents, [my] head, the school as in governing body . . . outside bodies like inspectors, educational thinking, government'. The compulsions Sarah felt were placed upon her by the wider society became a frequent topic of conversation during the research. She often expressed frustration at the contradictory messages between the didactic and interventionist style of teaching she felt society expected of her and what the research was telling her about more appropriate ways adults can develop children's learning. Through the research, Sarah felt she was now able to see 'clearly' that 'sometimes [intervention] is not a good thing . . . because sometimes the play or the talk that's going on stops because children want to make you happy and give you the answers that you want or what they think you want'. Sarah came to believe that she no longer had to perform in her customary role in order to maximise children's learning. Sarah's case is interesting, not only because she learned important lessons about appropriate adult interaction, but because she seems to have become consciously critical of the socially conventional power relationship between teacher and pupil. Her recognition of the untenable nature of the stereotypical authoritarian teacher role and her consequent adjustments in the way in which she related to her pupils imply that Sarah was embarking upon a more egalitarian form of practice. She learned to resist internalised social pressures to perform in the traditional way: 'I have seen how easy it is to intervene as an adult in the wrong way. I no longer feel guilty if I am in that area observing and not interacting. I need to observe before I can help the play'. Sarah came to learn that she did not have to conform to the typecast image of a 'teacher' constantly instructing pupils and directing their learning. She talked about how she had found the research 'so rewarding in that you could find out so much about [a] child' and that her findings were a 'revelation'. She came to develop a relationship with the children that was more child-centred in its approach in which the children could learn with rather than merely from their teacher.

(Rose, 2001)

The action research cycle

Action research

Action research provides practitioners with the means to confront the assumptions that underlie their practice and bring about perspective transformations of the self. Brookfield has noted that assumption hunting is not merely a reflective process, it also entails action – these points relate to those outlined earlier in this chapter about how reflection is also about *action*. He writes:

> As a process critical thinking is not purely passive. It involves alternating phases of analysis and action . . . This process of active inquiry combines reflective analysis with informed action. We perceive a discrepancy, question a given, or become aware of an assumption – and then we *act* upon these intuitions. As our intuitions become confirmed, refuted, or (most likely) modified through action, we hone and refine our perceptions so that they further influence our actions, become further refined, and so on.
>
> (Brookfield, 1987: 23)

Systematic critical reflection

Thinking about your practice may appear an automatic response, but it cannot be assumed to happen or left to chance. To be a Critical Reflector, you also need to be an *action researcher*. Noffke (1995: 5) argues that action research is about 'taking everyday things in the life of education and unpacking them for their historical and ideological baggage', and Kincheloe (1991: 122) contends that critical action researchers must 'dig out and expose to the light of day' hidden assumptions. In doing so, they will 'discover a world of personal meaning which is socially constructed by a variety of forces' (Kincheloe, 1991: 158). Action research is offered as a means by which reflection can acquire the focus and direction it needs. It can carry the reflection process a step further onto an active and deeper level, providing it with sufficient strength, structure, and purpose, beyond mere contemplation into an active investigation. Liston and Zeichner describe how it provides a practical agenda:

> It is . . . important to recognise that the self-reflective cycles of plan, act, observe, and reflect, occur naturally in the work of [practitioners]. The difference is that in action research [practitioners] conduct these activities more carefully and systematically than they normally would, and with somewhat more of a focus on particular issues over a period of time.
>
> (Liston and Zeichner, 1990: 246)

Action research can make critical reflection a *meaningful and realistic practice*. It turns what is otherwise an overwhelming multitude of thoughts and feelings about a myriad of acts into something that is both purposeful, and perhaps more importantly, manageable, for the busy practitioner. Action research takes the processes of both 'reflection in action' and 'reflection on action' a step further and helps to establish a long-term habit of self-examination.

The action research cycle

So what exactly is action research? Action research is a method of looking more closely at a particular aspect of practice by a process of *systematic investigation*. It is more than just reflecting 'in action' or reflecting 'on action' – it is the deliberate study of a particular issue of one's practice. This issue may be something that has arisen from a particular moment that occurred 'in action' – an exchange with a child that triggered a concern that you felt needed further exploration; or perhaps the focus results from a gradual and growing awareness that a particular aspect of provision is not working effectively; or it could be the need to review a policy in the light of new requirements that compels you to explore how this can be manifested in practice. Whatever the focus, undertaking an explicit examination of the chosen aspect should stimulate you to consider the underlying values and assumptions that inform and influence that aspect of practice, to question the effectiveness of your professional actions and judgements, and the impact these have on the children with whom you work. It enables you to look beyond the moment-by-moment daily reflections and assessments that already play a part.

With action research, reflection becomes a more deliberate and conscious process and has a more proactive and practical agenda. This increased insight can lead to better evaluations and more appropriate decisions about learning, thereby transforming the quality of children's experiences. Action research has been called 'critical praxis', since it turns critical reflection into practical action (Carr and Kemmis, 1986).

Looking through a different lens

An effective model of action research is to envisage it as a process of choosing a focus and then critically reflecting on that focus to ascertain how your practice can be improved upon. This can entail a practical investigation to gather more evidence or information to help understand the issue more clearly and help to resolve any problems. Such a practical investigation can many forms – it might involve doing observations, interviewing children or other adults, such as parents or members of staff, finding more information on a particular topic or reviewing relevant documentation. These are the different ways we can view the world from a different 'lens' as Brookfield (1995) has advocated – through the lens of a child, a parent, another practitioner or professional, a theorist, a government or the lens of your own experiences, which all help to make what might have been invisible, more visible. Whatever additional evidence might be necessary to deepen your awareness of the issue, the twin agendas of child-centred and socially just practices will always permeate your reflective process. After your research, you take action and implement whatever revised under-standing you now have on the issue. But your journey carries on as you continue to appraise new practices within a continuous spiral of improvement.

In addition to improving provision, action research can play an important part in re-enthusing and re-empowering you, as Case Study 1.1 shows. Through action research, you can be made to feel 'more professionally alive' and 'feel empowered to make significant changes in [your] profession' (Oja and Pine, 1987: 110). This helps to energize the 'critical spirit' necessary to motivate you to generate change. As a *change agent*, you can bring about more effectively child-centred and social justice practices, playing an active role in helping to ensure such practices are enacted. Certainly, the action research presented in the case studies here 'celebrate many small victories as well as personal learning, thereby continually building momentum for innovation toward a preferred future' (Bradbury, 2007: 292). As Zeichner (1993: 15) has predicted: 'While educational actions [by practitioners] cannot solve all . . . societal problems by themselves, *they can contribute their share to the building of more decent and just societies*' (emphasis in the original).

The Critical Reflector and learning communities

Collaborative action research

Many authors have expressed the possibility that action research may start small but can gradually widen to involve others and influence the setting's culture (see Rose, 2001). Action research provides a context for sharing common concerns of practical, real-world problems that are likely to attract interest and creates opportunities for collaborative inquiry. It has been argued that early years settings provide a natural context for collaborative research (Kelly and Rose, 1996) since they already share practice with several practitioners.

It is almost impossible for action research to be undertaken by an isolated individual, not least because it is about researching practice and is therefore always about interpersonal processes and relationships. It is also likely that the concerns of an individual practitioner or a focus on a particular child will always incorporate a consideration of the broader context, as has been argued earlier in this chapter. These processes invariably come into play given the multi-professional nature of many early years settings, particularly with the development of Sure Start centres, which may employ practitioners from a range of services. This opens up our own interpretations to new insights from those who might have different perspectives and helps to ensure a more holistic approach for the child (Craft and Paige-Smith, 2008).

A learning community

A 'learning community' essentially means that all the participants in the early years settings view themselves as lifelong learners and endeavour to share ideas and investigate their practice collaboratively, learning from and with each other. MacNaughton and Williams (2004) quote Fidler, who emphasizes the relational dimensions of a learning community:

> A group of colleagues who come together in a spirit of mutual respect, authenticity, learning and shared responsibility to continually explore and articulate an expanding awareness and base of knowledge. The process of learning community includes inquiring about each other's assumptions and biases, experimenting, risking, and openly assessing the results.
>
> (cited in MacNaughton and Williams, 2004: 226)

Even when critical reflection or action research begins as solitary self-evaluation, it is only the initial stage of a process that eventually involves sharing information and insights across and beyond the setting. In this way, common issues and concerns can be identified and developed and practices shaped by practitioners working together as a learning community. As such, they can develop 'some sense of shared meaning, ownership and even control over what is valued and recognised as appropriate practice' (Craft and Paige-Smith, 2008: 173). This may involve exposing and articulating differences, but engaging in debates helps to generate collective meaning making and more consistency in the adult role. So that even when various alternative interpretations of phenomena might abound, attempts can be made to synthesize perspectives through a communal critical approach and a common ground reached. All social contexts are filled with uncertainty and ambiguity, but if practitioners are prepared to reflect critically on their own professional knowledge, agreement can be reached, producing a continuum of consensus across and beyond the setting. But, as noted earlier in this chapter, any concordance reached is still subject to revision, since the quest for quality never ends.

Community of practice

Rogoff et al. (2001) have shown how collaborative participation with others in activities of common interest can create a learning community. This involves learning together through purposeful activities with mutual responsibilities and shared decision-making. These ideas are linked to the notion of a 'community of practice', which can be traced to Lave and Wenger (1991), who, like other socio-cultural theorists, highlighted the way in which all learning is socially situated and arises from our experiences of participating in daily life. In contrast to cognitive theorists who view learning in terms of the conceptual structures or forms of knowledge that evolve, Lave and Wenger focused on the different kinds of social engagements or relationships that provide a context and the means for learning to take place. Learning is a process of co-participation and we can learn by engaging in communities. The work of Lave and Wenger is useful for understanding how social groups (like early years practitioners) who have common interests and a shared focus can learn collaboratively and build practices together. Action research can help to provide a systematic way for the community of practice to improve provision and a means for enabling all practitioners to participate fully in the learning community, as Case Study 2.2 shows.

The idea of a learning community is facilitated by the 'oral craft tradition' that exists within settings in which stories about practice are shared between practitioners on a daily basis (Anderson et al., 1994). These social interactions and communicative exchanges have also been called 'naturally occurring narratives', which can be powerful vehicles for stimulating more deliberate investigations (Cortazzi, 1993). In undertaking action research within a learning community, the Critical Reflector will draw on different selves such as the Carer self, the Communicator self, and the Facilitator self to help propagate the caring, responsive, and meaningful relationships necessary for creating learning communities (MacNaughton and Williams, 2004). The last chapters of the book will show how practitioners draw on their Observer, Assessor, and Creator selves to carry out their research and improve their practice.

Children as co-researchers

In a learning community, all participants are active and children are part of the community of practice as much as adults. Evidence suggests that limited progress has been made in listening to the views of younger children and enabling their participation despite the ratification of the Convention of the Rights of the Child and government policies that have championed such principles (Alexander, 2010). The Critical Reflector can help to realize the rights of children's participation by perceiving them as *co-learners* in improving practice. There is a growing commitment in research that children's perspectives can and should be heard (Christensen and James, 2000; Rogers and Evans, 2008) and that children can be *co-researchers* (Moss, 2008). Developing learning communities and involving children directly in this process can increase children's sense of belonging and sense of identity, as they will feel fully accepted as part of the community (MacNaughton and Williams, 2004). Practical ways in which young children can be involved in improving practice are considered in Chapter 6, where we consider the methods adopted by the Mosaic approach (Clark and Moss, 2001).

Critically reflective connoisseurs

The early years setting provides a vibrant and powerful context for promoting community collaboration. Young children who attend may share the locality but come from a range of different cultural and socio-economic backgrounds. With action research, practitioners can become enterprising, independent learners and self-confident, critical thinkers who work consciously and continuously towards improving the quality of their practice. Through action research, they are provided with opportunities to develop their powers of understanding and are actively able to construct meaning in their educational practice, rather than passively to reproduce it. As they develop a more critical perspective of their practice, they will refine the art of becoming *educational connoisseurs* (Eisner, 1998) and become empowered to promote more egalitarian and just practices. If practitioners are learning, thinking, and feeling in this way, it is possible that children in their care will do the same, fulfilling their developmental promise and maximizing their prospects to help them to flourish in the society in which they live. To paraphrase Fullan (1993), practitioners must succeed if children are to succeed and children must succeed if society is to succeed.

Case study 2.2   Learning communities

The nursery where Andrew worked provides an example of the way in which the work of a single action researcher can have a broader effect on the rest of the setting and help to generate a learning community. He had decided to look at 'oracy' and how he supported children's talking. As part of this process, he tracked a group of children with whom he had been doing some cooking, who had decided to show the other members of staff what they had made. What happened is that every single practitioner asked the children the same kind of questions. His research showed how the teachers adopted the same didactic questioning style which tended to inhibit the children's responses. There was little discussion generated on the process of the cooking. The questions focused on the product of the cooking and did not enable the children to reflect on their experiences or communicate them beyond a single-word response. By the time the children had visited all the staff, Andrew felt that they were talking less than when they had first set out on their venture. His reflections on this evidence led Andrew to revise his initial understanding of children's oracy to be largely a matter of developmental capability to a more socio-cultural perspective as he began to comprehend the powerful impact that context can have in supporting children's communication. He discussed his findings during an informal conversation with a few of the other staff during a lunch break and this led to a more formal discussion at a staff meeting. When the evidence was reviewed the staff collectively realised that they were not only asking the children the same kind of questions, but their interactions were not developing the children's oracy skills. The work of one researcher triggered an evaluative response amongst colleagues as they began to challenge long established communicative styles they had erstwhile believed to be appropriate practice. For example, they decided to look more closely at the kinds of questions they asked children that were more open-ended and would elicit a more reflective response about processes and not just products. Andrew said: 'Just because we talked together about it, it changed it'. The action research had encouraged the setting to be a learning community working together to change practice for the better. What began as an investigation into children's communication became a revealing insight into how adults talk with children. Whilst some might view these events as a localised concern, it shows how small and evolving transformations within a community of practice can be significant because of the way they directly impact upon children's daily educative experiences. Although Andrew did not involve the children or their caregivers as co-researchers, these small changes in the way in which adults interact with young children have immediate implications for how children are treated which, in turn, have sociopolitical implications in terms of whether child-centred and socially just practices are pursued.

(Rose, 2001)

The Critical Reflector in adult-initiated and child-initiated activities

The quality of the relationship between adults and pupils and the style of practice that practitioners adopt is vitally important, with potential consequences for any stage of children's learning and development. As Critical Reflectors, we can ensure that provision is child-constructed rather than simply adult-imposed and that the curriculum is child-centred where active learning, participation, and 'finding out' are emphasized as much as 'being told', where the processes are as important as the products. Being a Critical Reflector will help practitioners to understand when to innovate and when to sustain existing practice, when to initiate an activity and when to be led by the child. By articulating their implicit belief system, by carefully examining any pre-judgements made of children's aptitudes, and by investigating the nature of their interactions, practitioners are more likely to develop a pedagogic role that is finely tuned into children's needs and interests and encompasses more proactive expectations of children's learning potential. They will recognize the uncertainty and ambiguity of the learning context but in the day-to-day interactions with young children, being a Critical Reflector will help them to reflect 'in' and 'on' their interactions and activities to ensure they are child-centred and socially just. By investigating their own practice within a learning community of practice, the Critical Reflector can be empowered to engender more worthwhile provision for all the children in their care.

Reflective questions and tasks

1. What do you think it means to have a 'critical spirit'?
2. Observe an adult and child interacting in a setting – think about whether the interactions reflect a child-centred and socially just pedagogy.
3. How would you ensure your reflections on practice incorporate a more critical stance?
4. Think of an early years setting that you know. Can you identify any features that show it to be a 'learning community' researching practice? What constraints and challenges exist in being a 'learning community'?

3   The Carer

To care for and be cared for are fundamental human needs.

(Nel Noddings)

The Carer self lies at the heart of the adult role and fundamentally underpins all early years practice. Historically, politically, and culturally, the notion of a Carer has not always been given the significance and respect it deserves. This chapter shows how being a Carer enables the adult to ensure that the child is given the essential nurturing environment to support the child's development and learning. Two key aspects are offered to clarify the nature of adult–child interactions when acting as a Carer: interactional synchrony and emotion coaching. These two forms of interaction are offered as the primary vehicles through which we can develop nurturing relationships, foster empathetic behaviour, and promote resilience in young children. We show how being a Carer has far-reaching implications for society as a whole and identify how the Carer self can help to engender child-centred and socially just practices.

The notion of a caring professional

The Carer dimension to the adult role recognizes that being a *caring professional* is an essential part of early years practice. Calls have been made for a 'culture of caring' and 'care-centred' practices, with caring being viewed as a 'central plank of professionalism' (Taggart, 2011: 85; see also Goldstein, 2002; McNamee et al., 2007). In England, the integral place of caring is also acknowledged by the Early Years Foundation Stage (EYFS), which devotes one of its four main principles (Positive Relationships) to developing caring relationships with children and their families. Two of its key commitments state clearly that children need to feel 'cared for' and that 'every interaction is based on caring professional relationships' (DfES, 2007: 2.1, 2.4). It also states that 'warm, trusting relationships' provide the basis for effective learning. The professional standards for Early Years Professional Status (EYPS) and Qualified Teacher Status (QTS) also require practitioners to establish respectful, trusting, supportive, and constructive professional relationships, encapsulating the idea of a caring professional (Q1, S25).

Nurturing relationships

The Carer is thus framed around the idea of a *nurturing relationship*, which is brought about by caring, trusting, and mutually respectful acts (Bronfenbrenner, 1979). A nurturing relationship is attentive, responsive, and gives thoughtful consideration to those who are cared for, providing the basis for lifelong caring attitudes (Brooker, 2010). It is something that you do with every interaction – it is about being 'care-full' rather than 'care-less' in the way we approach relationships (McNamee et al., 2007: 278). How we act as a Carer thus involves feeling concern for others, showing warmth, and displaying kindness. As Swick (2007: 97) puts it, 'the essential core of "caring" is about learning to love and nurture each other'. These processes are both co-constructed and co-dependent and thus the child is an active agent, and these ideas are explored more fully later in the chapter. However, caring can also be perceived in much broader terms – as more than just a feeling or an attribute – it is a 'moral act'.

A moral act and an ethic of care

Caring as a 'moral act' can be explained by the fact that our treatment of others carries moral overtones. This idea has been described in the literature as the 'ethic of care' and can be traced to the work of Noddings (1984, 1992), who viewed caring as a universal human concept and the foundation for making ethical decisions. Noddings (1984: 3) wrote that caring is 'the very wellspring of ethical behaviour' – such ethical behaviour includes acting on the basis of commonly held values that advocate respect, fairness, and decency towards others. An 'ethic of care' goes beyond conceiving caring merely as a maternal feeling to one that advocates care as a 'social principle' (Taggart, 2011). Viewed in this way, the personal and emotional aspects of caring are broadened to incorporate a perspective that recognizes that being a Carer has implications for social justice.

We saw in the Introduction how social justice practices include creating an egalitarian society in which all participants feel included and valued and are treated with dignity. It is about realizing the part that we can play in helping to promote an ethic of care. These views are shared by Swick (2007: 98), who claims that 'acts of caring . . . provide the entire community with a philosophy of caring that helps to raise the quality of life for everyone', a view also supported by Brooker (2010: 183), who states that caring gives rise to 'ethical politics and to notions of social justice and equality'. Viewed in this way, the Carer helps to create 'the nurturing rituals that engage children in finding decent and meaningful ways to live' (Swick, 2007: 98). Such 'nurturing rituals' can be realized through the adoption of *interactional synchrony* and *emotion coaching*, which are explained later in this chapter.

The idea of the Carer in supporting young children's experiences and understanding of social justice can be extended to enabling young children to participate effectively in their society and environment, thereby helping to sustain it. Noddings (1992) considers that the personal and early experiences of 'being cared about' and 'caring for' promote a wider application at a societal or global level. Through nurturing relationships and by setting norms of caring behaviour, the Carer can help young children to learn how caring 'works'. Siraj-Blatchford (2007) shares this vision, claiming that early years practitioners should be helping to prepare young children to participate and contribute to an inclusive global society and develop a 'cosmopolitan citizenship'. Research shows that from a very young age, children can internalize value-laden messages (Hyland, 2010) and it is the Carer who can help to ensure that such messages reflect a commitment to the welfare of others (Noddings, 1984). As Bronfenbrenner (1979: 53) suggests, 'no society can long sustain itself unless its members have learned the sensitivities, motivations, and skills involved in assisting and caring for other human beings', since children who experience caring, supportive relationships are more caring themselves in every aspect of their lives (Bronfenbrenner, 1979, 2005).

Interactional synchrony

One of the key ways in which the Carer can help to promote a nurturing relationship is through a process known as *interactional synchrony*. There are varying definitions of interactional synchrony and the notion was originally used to describe the way in which caregivers and infants appeared to imitate each other's movements, such as facial expressions or speech patterns, during interactions so that they appeared to be 'in sync'. In this book, interactional synchrony is considered more broadly to refer to the interpersonal relationship between caregiver and child in which the Carer sensitively *tunes into* the cared-for child in a responsive way that is 'in sync' with the child's needs and interests. It is a *reciprocal* and rewarding process for each partner, which helps to develop rapport but most importantly helps the child to feel socially connected and develop a sense of belonging.

There is a wealth of consistent evidence to suggest that interactional synchrony between caregiver and young child plays a significant role in promoting later development, such as attachment security, self-regulation, and advanced language (Feldman et al., 1999). Most of this research has focused its efforts on exploring the nature of interactional synchrony between parent and infant, but it is applicable to early years practitioners also, since they essentially replace the parent as caregiver when the child attends their setting. It has even greater significance when one considers the role that interactional synchrony appears to play in enabling secure *attachments* to exist between caregiver and child.

Attachment

Attachment essentially involves a *relational* process whereby a strong affectional tie develops between one person and another and is viewed as a biologically driven need for security. The theory of attachment, first proposed by Bowlby (1969), has undergone various revisions as more research has unearthed other dimensions to the process of attachment. For example, Bowlby's original assertion that attachment ought to take place between mother and child has been broadened to include any caregiver and it is now recognized that multiple attachments are possible (Schaffer and Emerson, 1964; Sroufe, 1995). Recognition of young children's capacity to attach to others is formalized in the Key Person role in England, which is now a statutory requirement for all early years settings in accordance with the EYFS (DfES, 2007). Recent neuroscientific evidence that appears to affirm the pivotal place of attachment in developing well-being has led to one part of the brain (the amygdala) being nicknamed 'Bowlby's bulb' (Brainethics, 2006).

Attempts have been made to ascertain the nature of attachment, and the various 'types' identified essentially differentiate between a secure and insecure attachment (Ainsworth et al., 1978). Insecure attachments manifest themselves in various forms (avoidant, resistant, and disorganized), but the complexities of these different forms of insecure attachments make diagnosis difficult, particularly as they are susceptible to cultural variations. What is apparent is the importance of secure attachment on later cognitive, emotional, and social development, which has been established by numerous studies (see Berk, 2003). Furthermore, there is evidence that the compensatory role of affectional ties can help counteract poor attachments, highlighting the role of the early years practitioner in providing a buffer zone for young children regardless of their parental relationships. Early years professionals can focus attention on those elements considered crucial to the development of healthy attachments such as envisaging themselves as a 'secure base' and 'safe haven'.

Secure base and safe haven

These notions were developed by Bowlby and are essentially embodied in the Carer acting as a designated Key Person for the child. A secure attachment with a Key Person provides young children with a secure base *to venture from* and playfully explore the environment, while the safe haven provides them with a *refuge* when that environment causes them any distress. In this way, the young child begins to negotiate the 'shifts between dependence, interdependence and independence' (Underdown, 2007: 48). The secure base/safe haven manifests itself for the child as both a physical and psychological base and haven so that the child feels not just 'what it is to feel good physically', but also 'to be cherished emotionally' (McNamee et al., 2007: 280).

Interactional synchrony

The secure base/safe haven is built through interactional synchrony, which essentially comprises *responsive communication* between caregiver and child. Berk (2003: 422) refers to this as an 'emotional dance' in which 'the caregiver responds to infant signals in a well-timed, rhythmic, appropriate fashion' and in which the infant responds to the emotional state of the caregiver. Cultural influences such as a social group's informal norms about when, where, and how one should express emotions (known as 'emotional display rules') will understandably help to define the nature of interactional synchrony but the main messages for the Carer are that interactions between caregivers and young children are bi-directional and co-regulated processes and are thus *contingent* – in other words, dependent upon each other.

Attunement

Interactional synchrony is thus a reciprocal process that is subtle and flexible and involves delicate 'tuning in' to develop a synchronous state of mutual understanding. Thus part of the process of interactional synchrony involves the idea of *attunement*. Drawing on the work of Winnicott and others, Underdown (2007: 36) describes how attunement helps to create secure attachments through the 'empathetic responsiveness' of the caregiver. Being emphathetically responsive means looking closely for verbal and non-verbal signals from the child that reflect how the child is feeling and what their needs and interests might be. This responsiveness might include the Carer recognizing when a child is being over-stimulated – the child might begin to cry – or when he or she has become bored by a particular stimulus – the child might look away. These signs or signals are not always obvious and may be expressed differently by different children. As Carers we can detect and learn from the signals given by a child and respond empathetically. Attunement is explored further in Chapter 4, which looks at the way in which caregivers communicate with children in helping to establish interactional synchrony.

Internal working models

The significance of interactional synchrony is borne out by numerous studies that have shown that consistent and appropriate responsiveness to children helps to develop attachment security (see, for example, De Wolff and van Ijzendoorn, 1997). This positive and responsive interaction with a caregiver provides an appropriate environment for a child to practise those skills that will help them to self-regulate their emotions, such as controlling their anger. These ideas are explored further in the next section. Interactional synchrony also helps to build what Bowlby (1988) called an *internal working model* of relationships. The internal working model refers to the cognitive structures that are formed through the young child's experiences of relationships. The nature and style of these relationships create a model of how the child views both self and others and influences the child's *expectations* regarding relationships and his or her responses to them, formulating a *framework for relationships*. An infant who receives consistent, responsive, attuned nurturing from his or her caregivers is most likely to develop a positive internal working model. In helping to establish an appropriate internal working model, interactional synchrony lays the foundation for all future relationships and mental health (Sroufe,1995; Fonagy et al., 2004).

Goodness-of-fit

A linked notion to interactional synchrony that can be accommodated into practice by the Carer is the goodness-of-fit model (Thomas and Chess, 1977). This means that the caregiver needs to adapt their child-rearing practices to suit the temperament of the child, particularly when they manifest more seemingly negative temperaments, rather than assuming a 'one-size-fits-all' model. Temperament is considered to be an innate disposition and so Carers need to make necessary adjustments in their responses to the child so that their responses 'fit' the child's temperament. This does not mean that we should indulge children's temperaments but that we work with the child to help them to function effectively in society. For example, so-called 'difficult' infants who receive positive and sensitive responses from caregivers, but who also encourage and support them in adjusting to new experiences, are more likely to have a diminished 'difficult' disposition (Feldman et al., 1999).

   While acknowledging the influence of cultural values in determining whether a child is 'difficult' or 'shy', the key message is that 'both difficult and shy children benefit from warm, accepting [caregiving] . . . that makes firm but reasonable demands for mastering new experiences' (Berk, 2003: 416). A goodness-of-fit approach has been shown to help foster more secure attachment and to prevent maladjustment in young children. Case Study 3.1 provides an example of how practitioners can generate interactional synchrony by tuning in sensitively and anticipating a young child's needs and interests.

Case study 3.1   Interactional synchrony

Sandra is a daycare practitioner and explained how interactional synchrony works in her carer role using the example of a new 6-month-old baby girl who had started at her daycare nursery. A consultation with the parent revealed various aspects about the child's routines and preferences but it was not until Sandra had spent some time 'tuning in' to the baby that Sandra was able to understand how best to promote the baby's well-being and development and help to ensure an attachment relationship. Sandra describes the kinds of interactions she had with the new baby:

I carefully watched and listened to the baby's responses to the nursery routine, both her verbal and non-verbal actions, and then I was able to see which aspects the baby found difficult and which aspects the baby appeared to enjoy. During 'play time', I made sure I engaged in eye contact whenever possible and took turns with the baby by having reciprocal 'conversations'. I mimicked the sounds the baby made and copied her facial expressions, following the baby's lead. Sometimes I initiated an interaction such as singing a song or talking to her, but I always checked to see if she was responsive to my engagement with her. I tried to share the baby's interests or what I thought she was interested in but I also carefully and gently introduced new possibilities when I thought she was receptive to new stimulation. I watched carefully for signs of 'habituation', as I know this usually means the baby is bored with a particular toy or game and needs a new distraction. Sometimes this expresses itself with signs of distress and I have to keep checking to see if the behaviour exhibited means that the baby is tiring of new stimulation and in danger of being over-stimulated. These signs can vary from baby to baby and so I have to get to know what expressions or sounds or movements they make mean 'I want a new toy' or 'I'm tired and just need a cuddle'. I learned from this baby that a small whimpering noise meant that she'd had enough stimulation but that turning away and frowning meant that she was bored. I also discovered that she did not enjoy being changed and so I knew that she needed additional reassurance and interaction, which helped to distract her from her discomfort. I made sure the other staff were aware of her sensitivity to being changed so that they could also ensure that they provided the necessary interactions when she was being changed.

These kinds of sensitive interactions helped Sandra to build an 'emotional dialogue' and to 'tune in' to the baby, developing a sense of 'togetherness' based on mutual expectation and trust. This built up an attachment relationship and helped the new baby to feel safe and secure. The process of attunement was sometimes initiated by the baby and sometimes by Sandra, but was always sensitive to the baby's needs and desires.

Emotion coaching

Closely aligned with the process of interactional synchrony is emotion coaching. Emotion coaching is integral to the Carer, since it involves the accommodation of a young child's feelings. All infants innately express the basic (and universal) emotions of happiness, surprise, interest, fear, anger, sadness, and disgust. By about the age of 2 years, secondary or 'self-conscious' emotions emerge such as pride, envy, guilt, and shame, although the development of these secondary emotions (also known as higher-order feelings) is far more culturally dependent. The interactions between caregiver and child fundamentally affect the development of both universal and secondary emotions, particularly the latter, in how they are expressed, experienced, and managed. Goleman (1995) has shown how during the first three or four years of life 'emotional learning' occurs more readily than later in life. Thus, although the cultural context plays a role in the development of emotions, the caregiver role in supporting infants' and young children's regulation of all their emotions (both basic and self-conscious) remains critical, because the infant is so dependent on the caregiver for help in managing the basic emotions, and because cultural expectations and feedback help to determine the nature and intensity of the self-conscious emotions. As LeDoux puts it, 'we come into the world capable of being afraid and capable of being happy, but we must learn which things make us afraid and which make us happy' (cited in Geake, 2009: 116).

Acceptance of feelings

The work of John Gottman (Gottman et al., 1996; Gottman and DeClaire, 1997) has highlighted the importance of the Carer *accepting young children's feelings* – what Rogers called 'unconditional positive regard' (cited in Roberts, 2002) – an acceptance that is independent of their behaviour. Gottman first introduced the notion of emotion coaching, which offers an alternative perspective on caregiver style. Gottman's approach emphasizes the process of emotional regulation rather behaviour modification – in other words, a focus on the feelings that ultimately drive the behaviour rather than the behaviour itself. Gottman has shown that much of the child-rearing theories and popular advice that abound in childcare practices, both inside and outside the home, focus on addressing children's misbehaviour and 'disregard the feelings that underlie that misbehaviour' (Gottman and DeClaire, 1997: 16).

Meta-emotion

Emotion coaching involves the development of meta-emotion – the 'organised set of feelings and cognitions about one's own emotions and the emotions of others' (Gottman and DeClaire, 1997: 7). Meta-emotion is essentially your personal views and beliefs about emotions and what they mean to you and how aware you are of these. It includes how you value emotions, in what ways or contexts you think they ought to be expressed (or not!), and how you ought to respond to them. Emotions are invariably influenced by the emotion display rules of your particular socio-cultural context. An emotion coaching style of caregiving (also known as parental meta-emotion philosophy) reflects the capacity to be both aware of our own emotions as well as those of children, and to utilize 'meta-emotion' (awareness of emotions) to benefit children's socialization and assist them in the nurturing of their emotional well-being, particularly during instances of negative behaviour. According to Gottman et al. (1996), such an approach is associated with better emotional regulation and more competent problem-solving. Emotion coaching also correlates well with higher self-esteem, better academic success, and more positive peer relations (Gottman et al., 1996). In contrast, caregiving that is ineffective in addressing the emotional dimensions of children's development has more negative outcomes (Hooven et al., 1995; Katz et al., 1996).

Empathy and guidance

Freeman and Vakil (2007: 274) claim that the development of pro-social engagement is a primary responsibility of early years professionals and that they ought to 'take advantage of opportune moments to teach appropriate behaviour'. This is possible via the adoption of emotion coaching in practice, which essentially consists of two key elements: *empathy* and *guidance*. These two elements express themselves through various processes that caregivers undertake whenever 'emotional moments' occur. These involve recognizing, labelling, and validating the young child's emotions, regardless of the behaviour, so as to promote self-awareness of emotions. The circumstances might also require setting limits on appropriate behaviour (such as stating clearly what is acceptable behaviour) and possible consequential action (such as implementing behaviour management procedures), but key to this process is engagement with the child in problem-solving to support the child's ability to learn to self-regulate.

In this way, the child's safe haven/secure base and sense of acceptance is maintained, while the boundaries of inappropriate behaviour are clearly communicated. The child and adult work together to seek alternative courses of action to help manage emotions and prevent future transgressions. The problem-solving dimension to emotion coaching is similar to that taken by the High/Scope approach, which originated in America. In High/Scope kindergartens, social conflict is resolved by encouraging discussion with adults and other children (OECD, 2004). Clearly, this process is adaptable and responsive to the developmental capabilities of the child, with the adult scaffolding pro-social solutions. Strategies are increasingly adopted by young children as they develop their language capabilities and ability to organize their thoughts, which might include being able to make alternative choices (Thompson, 1990). By enabling children to problem-solve solutions that will help them to manage their feelings and the behavioural consequences of those feelings, the child is engaged in managing their behaviour – in these respects, emotion coaching is a child-centred practice. Over time, this promotes a sense of empowerment, self-control, and resilience. In effect, emotion coaching techniques instil the tools that will aid children's ability to regulate their behaviour and emotions – what is known as *reflective self-functioning* (Music, 2010).

Attuning to children's emotions

Emotion coaching is validated by research on the importance of 'attunement', whereby the caregiver lets the child know his or her emotions are met with empathy, are accepted, and (if appropriate) reciprocated, and thus forms part of the process of interactional synchrony. As Goleman (1995: 100) notes, 'countless repeated moments of attunement or misattunement between [caregiver] and child shape the emotional expectations adults bring to their close relationships'. The process of attunement creates an emotional connection and provides reassurance to the child as he or she learns about the causes, consequences, and behavioural signs of emotions in increasingly complex ways and at the same time develops an ability to 'interpret, predict and change others' feelings' (Berk, 2003: 405).

Roberts (2002: 12) talks about the importance of accepting all feelings in developing self-esteem and says that acceptance is 'at the heart of self-concept'. It is in our responses to emotional displays that adults give 'signals' about our approval and acceptance. Rejection of feelings such as sadness leads to children 'excluding' them from their perception of themselves, leading them to 'lose' such feelings in order to be acceptable. Instead of ignoring, dismissing or trying to control young children's emotions, Gottman suggests that we need to engage with and validate emotions to show that all feelings are acceptable, *but* at the same time help children to understand that the ways in which they are expressed may not be.

Emotional intelligence

Gottman's work builds on the concept of emotional intelligence and the importance of developing emotional literacy that has been popularized by Goleman (1995). The term 'emotional intelligence' was first coined by Salovey and Mayer, who later defined it as:

the ability to perceive accurately, appraise, and express emotion; the ability to access and/or generate feelings when they facilitate thought; the ability to understand emotion and emotional knowledge; and the ability to regulate emotions to promote emotional and intellectual growth.

(Salovey and Mayer, 1990: 10)

Goleman (1995: 6) highlights how the term emotion is derived from the Latin verb 'to move', emphasizing that emotions 'are, in essence, impulses to act'. Goleman's work has drawn attention to the 'emotional mind', which he claims is a powerful 'system of knowing' that feeds into and informs the operations of the rational mind. In turn, the rational mind can refine and sometimes veto the input of the impulsive emotional mind *but only if it learns to do this*. He notes how the 'thinking' brain grew out of the emotional brain and that 'there was an emotional brain long before there was a rational one' (Goleman, 1995: 10). Since emotions are instinctive automatic responses and often based on a databank of emotional memories, we literally 'feel before we think' (Boyatzis, cited in Orme, 2001).

Emotional highjacking

Why is emotion coaching a potentially important strategy for the early years professional? Put simply, emotional memories are stored in that part of the brain called the amygdala (which you may recall has been labelled 'Bowlby's bulb'), which is responsible for giving meaning to sensory information. Sensory information (visual, auditory, olfactory) is sent first to the amygdala *before* being processed in the decision-making areas of the brain (the frontal cortex). If the sensory information is determined by the amygdala to be a real or imagined threat, it signals to the rest of the body to mobilize it into a 'fight and flight' response. The amygdala has the power to influence how the rest of the brain functions, including the centres for rational thought, since emotional outbursts are instinctive and unconscious and cannot be prevented – our emotions literally have a 'mind of their own'. Goleman (1995) refers to the 'fight and flight' response as 'emotional highjacking'. We now know that the same neural pathways are used for both an actual experience and the remembrance of an event and that

endangerment can be signaled not just by an outright physical threat but also, as is more often the case, by a symbolic threat to self-esteem or dignity: being treated unjustly or rudely, being insulted or demeaned, being frustrated in pursuing an important goal.

(Goleman, 1995: 60)

Since we no longer live in a society in which danger is ever present, the role of those parts of the brain that provide a more analytic and appropriate response to perceived danger becomes more important to allow for greater discernment in emotional responses and subsequent behaviour.

The role of the vagus nerve

So while we are unable to prevent emotional responses, what we are able to do is to help to control how long they last and how well regulated they are. To reverse the 'fight and flight' response, a part of the brain known as the vagus nerve needs to be stimulated. The vagus nerve connects with every major organ of the body and has a vital role in regulating involuntary responses. Gottman has shown that emotion coaching has a positive impact on the operation of the vagus nerve, since the techniques of emotion coaching trigger the vagus nerve into helping the body calm down and enabling the child to develop what is known as 'high vagal tone' (Gottman et al., 1996). It is this capacity to develop high vagal tone that appears to directly affect our well-being and responses to stress in later life (Goleman, 1995; Gottman et al., 1996). Although young children's brains and nervous systems are still under construction, it is of particular importance for the Carer to help support them in developing high vagal tone: 'Just as kids with good muscle tone excel at sports, kids with high vagal tone excel at responding to and recovering from emotional stress' (Gottman and DeClaire, 1997: 39).

Young children who are in an emotional state *need to be calmed down* before they are able to respond to reasoning. Since feelings are self-justifying, the Carer needs to get 'in sync' with the child by affirming the existence of their feelings. This process triggers the vagus nerve to self-soothe. Once the child has calmed down, they are more open to reasoning and the Carer is then able to work with the child in creating effective neural connections to the frontal cortex to become an 'efficient manager of emotion' (Goleman, 1995: 26). Such a process is of great significance if young children are to progress their learning, since emotional highjacking interferes with attentional processes and the ability to learn (Geake, 2009). As Blakemore and Frith (2005: 179) put it, 'a learner needs to be emotionally competent for optimal learning to occur'.

Emotional self-regulation

The capacity to recover helps to develop a sense of 'self-efficacy', which Goleman (1995: 89) describes as 'the belief that one has mastery over the events of one's life and can meet challenges when they come up'. Berk (2003) highlights how cognition and emotion are viewed as being in a 'bidirectional relationship', with emotions serving as both a motivation for and an outcome of mastery. This has close links with Dweck and Leggett's (1988) perspective of developing 'mastery' learning dispositions in children rather than a sense of helplessness. What emotion coaching can do is help young children develop strategies to adjust their emotional states to a comfortable intensity so that they can accomplish their goals. Emotional self-regulation paves the way for emotional self-efficacy and 'fosters a favourable self-image and an optimistic outlook' (Berk, 2003: 403). This in turn fosters a positive disposition to learning, which is discussed further in Chapter 8 (see Katz and Chard, 1989).

The process of emotion coaching

Emotion coaching provides the Carer with strategies to help children to self-regulate their emotions:

- by triggering a calmer response through empathetic support;
- by assisting young children to self-soothe by raising their awareness of their own emotional state and helping them to establish good vagal tone;
- by using the emotional moment as an opportunity to scaffold the young children's self-management of their emotions and behaviour.

Emotional blueprints

Goleman (1995: 22) notes how 'the interactions of life's earliest years lay down a set of emotional lessons based on the attunement . . . between infant and caretakers'. Such early *emotional blueprints* stored as emotional memories in the amygdala can be likened to Bowlby's internal working model.

Emotion coaching offers one possible strategy for adults to help children to self-regulate their behaviour. In England, the EYFS endorses an emotion coaching style of interaction by the Carer. It states that adults 'need to empathise with children and support their emotions' and claims '[w]hen children know that their feelings are accepted they learn to express them, confident that adults will help them with how they are feeling' (DfES, 2007: 3.3). In reference to the Personal, Social, and Emotional Area of Development, the EYFS states that '[c]hildren who are encouraged to feel free to express their ideas and their feelings, such as joy, sadness, frustration and fear, can develop strategies to cope with new, challenging or stressful situations' (DfES, 2007: 4.4), which in turn highlight the importance of developing resilience and generating empathetic attitudes in young children. These ideas are explored further in the remainder of this chapter.

Case study 3.2   Emotion coaching

Bonnie is a Reception teacher in an inner city primary school in London who has used emotion coaching techniques in her practice. She found emotion coaching particularly helpful with a difficult 5-year-old girl who was prone to temper tantrums. In her frustration, this child sometimes damaged property such as tearing down displays on the walls. Initially, Bonnie responded with a style of inter-action which Gottman calls 'Disapproving'. When adults adopt this kind of response, they do so with a disciplinarian stance that is invariably critical of both the emotions and the behaviour. Bonnie instinctively adopted this role, as she felt it was expected of her as a teacher and tried to control the girl's reactions with reprimands and threats. At other times, Bonnie found herself adopting what Gottman calls a 'Dismissing' style of interaction with the girl, which meant that she either ignored or trivialized the girl's negative emotions such as telling her that she was 'being silly' and 'making a big deal out of nothing'. Eventually, Bonnie realized that neither disapproving nor dismissing the child's emotions and behaviour was preventing the tantrums from occurring and so she decided to follow Gottman's advice and adopt an 'Emotion Coach' style of interaction. The next time the girl had a tantrum, instead of getting cross with her or ignoring her, Bonnie said things like 'You seem to be feeling angry. I can see that you are feeling fed up. Shall we talk about how you're feeling?' If the child's emotions were resulting in a particular problem, such as damaging property, Bonnie would include limit-setting state-ments such as 'I can see you are cross now but it's not OK to rip that display or push that girl. I need to help you to feel calm so that you don't hurt anything'. By empathizing with the girl's feelings, Bonnie stopped the tantrum from getting worse, almost as if it 'took the wind out of her sails'. When the girl was feeling calmer, Bonnie was able to talk about how she could manage her feelings better and they worked together to think of some ways they could prevent the feelings from causing misbehaviour. The girl did not respond immediately the first time Bonnie tried emotion coaching but it did seem to calm her more quickly. Bonnie also said that initially she had some misgivings about trying emotion coaching, as she was concerned that it would diminish her authority and that the empathy would make things worse by legitimizing the behaviour. But as Bonnie came to realize that emotion coaching also enables the adult to set limits about appropriate behaviour, she was able to help the girl to realize that it was her feelings that were causing the behaviour and that this distinction gave both Bonnie and the girl a means to communicate more effectively and to learn to co-regulate both the girl's feelings and her behaviour. Over time, the girl learnt to recognize when she was feeling angry or frustrated and started to verbalize her feelings rather than lashing out. She also started to use some of the ideas she and Bonnie had discussed to help manage her behaviour. Instead of reacting and getting more angry whenever something frustrated her, she would say: 'I'm feeling cross and so I'm going to go and sit down now in my special calming place'. The girl had learnt to self-soothe, prevent escalation of her feelings, and moderate her behaviour more effectively – she had acquired reflective self-functioning.

Resilience

Since young children whose caregivers talk about feelings have a greater capacity to judge others' emotions at an older age (Dunn et al., 1991; Gottman and DeClaire, 1997), the adoption of interactional synchrony and emotion coaching resonates closely with the literature on resilience. This literature has highlighted the importance of social relationships and social skills in counteracting adversity such as socio-economic disadvantage (Smith et al., 2004). The notion of *resilience* refers to the process of being able to cope with exposure to negative events and circumstances and demonstrate positive adjustment in the face of trauma (Bartley, 2006). Opportunities for individuals to experience social and emotional support, recognize their strengths and capabilities, and develop positive social skills, promote feelings of competence and self-belief and support positive planning for the future (Kumpfer et al., 2010). We now know that an adult, other than family members, who forms a special relationship with a child can promote resiliency. Although temperament and other factors play a role in promoting young children's capacity to adapt effectively in the face of adversity, it is clear that early years practitioners as Carers can help to 'inoculate' children against the negative effects of adversity (Berk, 2003).

Other resilience studies have also shown how a warm and supportive adult–child relationship can buffer the effects of poverty and can act as the strongest moderating effect on the behaviour of children from poor families (Jones and Schoon, 2008). Research suggests that children can learn resilient thinking patterns from a very young age, which can optimize the development of resilience (Seligman et al., 1995). Such resilient thinking skills equate with the idea of *reflective self-functioning*, which was mentioned earlier. A significant aspect of such success includes operating within a context of nurturing and emotionally supportive relationships (Klein and Knitzer, 2006) that the Carer can create.

Developing empathy

Fostering empathy

We have outlined how the process of nurturing relationships in the early years setting can be aided through interactional synchrony and emotion coaching strategies and that these can, in turn, support the development of resilience in young children. At the core of nurturing relationships is the process of fostering empathy. Empathy involves a complex interaction of cognition and affect. It includes the ability to detect different emotions, to take another person's perspective. But more than that, it includes the ability to *'feel with* that person, or respond emotionally in a similar way (Berk, 2003: 407, original emphasis). In the early years, we need to help support young children's attunement to emotions, since 'the root of caring, stems from the capacity of empathy' (Goleman, 1995: 96) and can be encouraged by building self-awareness, which in turn builds skills in reading others' emotions.

Theory of mind

Empathy is inextricably linked to children developing a *theory of mind*. This is the ability to recognize and understand that others have beliefs, views, and intentions that are different from your own. Put simply, it is the capacity to put yourself in someone else's shoes and relies on social experiences to help bring it to fruition. Theory of mind is also known as 'mentalizing', but Sacha-Cohen offers a more familiar term – 'empathizing' (Blakemore and Frith, 2005). Although some research suggests that it is not until children are about four years of age that they have an established theory of mind, neuroscientific evidence reveals the existence of *mirror neurons*, which can be activated in our brains from a very early age. These mirror neurons are nerve cells in the brain that are activated simply by watching others do something or behave in a certain way. A simple example is when an adult picks up a glass of water and drinks from it. The mirror neurons in the brain of a baby watching this action will also activate those parts of the brain that are necessary to undertake that action, even though the baby cannot physically do it. This remarkable finding from neuroscience shows that even when we are unable to perform an action ourselves, our brain can still 'mimic' the action internally.

Other research has shown similar activation when we watch someone getting hurt. Our mirror neurons activate a similar response in our brain even though we might not be physically hurt. It is now believed that these mirror neurons appear to play a role in developing empathy and more effective socializing by enabling us to 'read' others' minds (Blakemore and Frith, 2005; Geake, 2009) – in other words, to develop a theory of mind. We know, for example, that a child as young as 1 can feel distress when she sees another child cry, challenging the egocentric perspective held by Piaget and others that young children are unable to view the world from another perspective (Goleman, 1995).

A moral being

Empathy also appears to play an integral role in becoming a 'moral being' (Berk, 2003). Moral behaviour is concerned with feelings such as empathy that help us to make judgements about whether actions are right or wrong. Such judgements are influenced by social understanding and cultural norms about what is acceptable or unacceptable behaviour. Good opportunities for applying emotion coaching techniques to support children's moral, prosocial behaviour arise when young children behave antisocially such as pushing another child or trying to take another child's toy – a common enough occurrence in any early years setting. An adult can empathize with both the perpetrator and the victim. Empathy with the perpetrator helps them to understand their own feelings and to calm down – but does not condone the behaviour. Empathy with the victim reassures the child, but also helps the perpetrator to see that others have feelings too. During an emotion-coaching moment like this, caregivers are able to call upon the child's own feelings to generate connections with how other people can have the same feelings as they do. This opens up opportunities to generate empathy and insight into the consequences of their actions on others. At the same time, the caregiver communicates acceptable social behaviour so that the child learns the 'rules' of the socio-cultural environment and begins to understand the reasons behind adults' behavioural expectations.

Social justice

Young children can actively construct concepts of justice and fairness via their emotional experiences and social interactions with the world. A *sense of justice* appears to play an important role in moral development and formulates early in toddlerhood – young toddlers are able to ascertain when something is 'not fair', such as when sweets are shared unequally – social justice in action. What is important is how we support such development given the implications for social justice. Gilligan (1982) claims that moral consciousness should not only focus on rights and justice but also on care and responsiveness. Her perspective draws on the 'ethic of caring' discussed earlier and the importance of empathy.

The development of empathy thus has important implications for Carers in promoting social justice. Empathy is an 'important motivator of prosocial, or altruistic, behaviour' (Berk, 2003: 407). Children develop understanding of moral conduct from an early age through their social interactions (Blakemore and Frith, 2005) and lay the foundations for what Hoffman (2000) regards as the most mature form of empathy – generalized concerns for social justice issues such as poverty and oppression. This can help to break down biased stereotypes, foster tolerance, compassion, and acceptance of difference and inclusive perspectives, all of which ought to be integral goals for the Carer. For as Swick notes:

If we truly internalize caring as a way of thinking we become stewards of our world. We examine how we live with others and our care of the environment. We are more in tune with how our lives impact the lives of others . . . [and] determines the kind of society we can have.

(Swick, 2007: 97)

The Carer in adult-initiated and child-initiated activities

The establishment of nurturing relationships through interactional synchrony and emotion coaching will help the Carer to tune into the child's needs and interests. Being 'in sync' will help to determine the nature of adult involvement and the degree of direction required. For example, a directly interventionist approach may help counter negative behavioural incidents. However, even in these cases, an emotion coaching style of interaction immediately turns the exchange into a process of co-regulation, mutual empathy, and shared problem-solving and helps the child to develop reflective self-functioning. Should the adult deem it appropriate to initiate a particular activity with young children based on prior exchanges, they will always apply the principles of interactional synchrony so that the activity immediately becomes a responsive, reciprocal, and interactive process. The attributes and actions that are proposed in this chapter in relation to the Carer dimension of the adult role can be applied to all interactions and activities with young children.

Reflective questions and tasks

1. Consider how you might establish an 'ethic of care' in an early years setting.
2. What factors might inhibit you from developing an emotion coaching approach in your practice?
3. Look at the behaviour policy in an early years setting and evaluate whether this policy reflects any of the characteristics of the Carer outlined in this chapter.
4. What do you think 'moral behaviour' should entail?

4   The Communicator

The way we communicate with others and with ourselves ultimately
determines the quality of our lives.

(Anthony Robbins)

The main aim of this chapter is to generate understanding not simply of how
early years practitioners help young children to communicate, but how they
communicate themselves. Effective communication forms a fundamental part
of the early years practitioner's role and arguably drives the entire process. This
chapter draws attention to some of the complexities of the communicative
process and ways in which the Communicator can help to build child-centred
and socially just practices. This is framed around the idea of connecting with
others and highlights the important and multisensory elements of the communicative act that early years practitioners should consider in their interactions
with children and other people. Central to this connecting process are the
notions of 'metalinguistic awareness', 'attunement', 'inter-subjectivity', and
especially the recognition of the power of non-verbal communication – all of
which are explored in this chapter. The importance of the 'child's voice' is
recognized and acknowledgement is made of the many different way in which
children can communicate meaning, although particular attention is paid to
verbal and non-verbal communications with young children in the day-to-day
work of early years settings and how adults can support language development. In doing so, we highlight the co-constructive and reciprocal nature of
communication.

The art of communication

Connecting with others

As a Communicator, we view communication not just as a two-way exchange
of information or a skill that is developed, but as being about *connecting with*

others and that this connection manifests in many forms. The drive for humans to connect with each other is apparent within hours of birth when it is possible to see newborns imitate the facial expressions and hand movements of a caregiver (Trevarthan, 1993). Whitehead (2002: 4) refers to these early signs of communication as a drive to get 'in touch with another mind'. Moreover, newborns will also initiate communication via eye-gazing and terminate it by looking away, proactively engaging in the communicative act from the outset (Berk, 2003). The drive for connecting with others is supported by socio-cultural theory, which emphasizes the impact of the socio-cultural context on all human development and learning. A notable example is the work of Vygotsky (1986), who paid particular attention to the way in which language develops. For Vygotsky (1978: 88), 'human learning presupposes a specific social nature' and children acquire language by observing and interacting with their cultural group. In this way, children learn to use the 'cultural tools' of their society, with language the ultimate 'cultural tool'.

According to Vygotsky, communicative exchanges with the social world shape young children's cognitive development as they internalize language and use it as a tool for shaping thinking. Vygotsky wrote: 'we become ourselves through others' (cited in Morgan, 2010: 18). Socio-cultural theory emphasizes how learning is the result of participation in socio-cultural practices and is thus socially and culturally co-constructed through collaborative relationships and interactions with others driven by an innate need to *connect*. Put simply, we learn by communing with and connecting to others. The Communicator might just as easily be named the Connector.

Multi-modal communication

Connecting with others is not simply a matter of speaking and listening, reading or writing, as formal curricular frameworks such as the Early Years Foundation Stage (EYFS) might lead us to believe; it is also about exchanging meaning, responding, understanding, and establishing relationships in a reciprocal and complementary manner. As early years practitioners, you will notice that young children communicate in a variety of ways not only through spoken language and body language but also in their playful activities, which include mark-making, junk-modelling, role-play, singing, and so forth. Drawing on the work of Kress, Worthington (2007) refers to these different ways or 'modes' of making meaning as 'multi-modalities' and we will explore young children's multi-modal activities in Chapter 6. But in terms of being a Communicator, the early years practitioner can embrace the art of communi-cation in its broadest sense, including recognizing the powerful role of non-verbal communication in helping to connect with others. Non-verbal communication (or the *paralinguistic* features of communication) is explored later in this chapter.

Metalinguistic awareness

Another dimension to the art of communication is incorporating what is known as *metalinguistic awareness*, or the ability to think about language as a system or to deliberately reflect on its use and its conventions. Metalinguistic awareness is mostly associated with developmental theory related to language development in children and their capacity to develop awareness of, for example, *grammatical rules* (the way in which words are arranged and used in sentences), *semantics* (the meaning of words), and *phonology* (rules governing the structure and sequence of speech sounds). *Pragmatics* is another important dimension to metalinguistic awareness, since it highlights the importance of *context* in communication. Pragmatic awareness refers to the socio-cultural rules of engaging in effective communication, which includes turn-taking, stating meaning clearly, using gestures, and tone of voice – these processes might appear straightforward but we are sure all readers can recall a conversation in which turn-taking might have been lacking or a harsh tone of voice was used that inhibited your response.

Socio-cultural dimensions deepen the complexity of pragmatic awareness when taking into consideration adjustments that might be necessary regarding interaction rituals across socio-cultural groups, such as various ways of greeting, or the way in which social relationships affect how we communicate, such as changing the way we talk with different age or status groups. (Together with paralinguistics, the process of pragmatic awareness is discussed further on pp. 59–60.)

In children, metalinguistic awareness begins to emerge more consciously from around the age of 3–5 years, but we have applied the notion of metalinguistic awareness to the Communicator more broadly. In addition to our knowledge and understanding of young children's linguistic development, metalinguistic awareness can alert us to be more conscious of language and its use. Such metalinguistic awareness includes an acknowledgement that language can be a powerful tool for the mind and foster cognitive development. Such a view embraces recent evidence, for example, that overturns deficit perspectives of bilingual learners and instead respects the many positive attributes bilingualism appears to engender, including greater cognitive flexibility, improved selective attention and analytical reasoning; so much so that it has been suggested that all children should become bilingual, 'thereby fostering the cognitive, language, and cultural enrichment of the entire nation' (Berk, 2003: 388).

Communication and the current political and legal context

Statutory obligations

The importance of communication is recognized in the EYFS as the Communication, Language, and Literacy Area of Learning (soon to be Communication and Language with Literacy forming a sub-level). Communication is also invariably upheld as the most important skill that any professional (or any human for that matter) can acquire. The EYPS and QTS Standards both incorporate several standards relating to communication, in terms of the practitioners' own communicative skills and their role in supporting the communication skills of children. Among the range of communicative functions outlined in the Standards, early years practitioners and teachers are judged on their capacity to be sensitive, empathetic, respectful, and positive communicators. Communication also heads the list of core skills and knowledge expected of adults working with children, known as the 'Common Core' (CWDC, 2010). Communication is considered central in work with young children and their families and statutory requirements confirm its key role in establishing and maintaining relationships.

The importance of literacy

The emphasis given to communication is unsurprising given its foundational implications for literacy. Reading and writing in western cultures is paramount. The emphasis given to literacy skills by government educational policy in the UK, both past and present, is an example of the way cultural beliefs determine what is expected from children and how communities directly influence what is learned (Rogoff, 1990). This idea also links with the work of Bourdieu (1977), who noted how literacy is a form of 'cultural capital', since the ability to read and write can ultimately be converted into wealth, social status, and social mobility. Yet there is growing concern regarding apparent 'language impoverishment' in children under the age of 5, with research showing how this affects school progress and life-chances (see, for example, DCSF, 2008a). This is the impetus behind some of the previous government's initiatives such as the Primary National Strategy framework and Every Child a Talker, as well as the current government's plan to introduce reading tests at age 6 – all aimed at improving literacy. Much of the concern has centred on young children's reading capabilities with particular attention being paid to the development of phonology or *phonological awareness*. We saw earlier that phonology forms part of the process of meta-linguistic awareness. It is the ability to recognize different segments of words by the different sounds they make – this might include recognizing that

certain words rhyme with each other. There is evidence to suggest that phonological awareness is the 'most accurate predictor of reading achievement'
(Barratt-Pugh and Rohl, 2000: 6).

This research led the previous government to implement pedagogical
strategies to ensure that practitioners facilitate phonological awareness in
young children. How adults do this is a subject of much controversy and is
known as the 'Phonics debate', with some advocating formal teaching of
phonic knowledge (Rose, 2006). But literacy experts such as Whitehead (2007)
have warned against over-simplifying this process and relying on the use of
particular strategies – she refers to the 'literacy iceberg', which reveals a hidden
mass of multiple experiences of sharing stories, singing nursery rhymes,
encounters with environmental print, and such like, all of which contribute to
young children's growing literacy. She also highlights the most important
ingredient of all, namely 'adult responsiveness', as the following sections
demonstrate.

The development of attunement

Attunement

The Carer chapter introduced the notion of attunement and how it is essentially about creating a harmonious and responsive relationship. It involves
being fully aware of the child in every way *in the moment* and adapting our
interactions to suit the child's receptivity to them. Attunement involves
'tuning in' to a child and altering our responses to suit that particular
child's developmental and personal needs and interests. Tuning into a child
requires sensitive interpretation of the child and context and an empathetic
attitude to help improve the quality of the communicative exchange. It
bears many of the hallmarks of 'interactional synchrony' and is thus as much
about co-regulation as building rapport. It also helps to establish trust and
respect, generate genuine interest and consideration of others, and create
possibilities for more open dialogue. Siegel (1999: 117) describes attunement
as 'collaborative, contingent communication'.

Co-regulation

In essence, the attunement process is both complex and subtle and comprises
various strategies that help the caregiver to tune into a young child's signals
and cues. Underdown (2007) cites the example of a caregiver responding to a
'hunger cry' and, in doing so, the various messages that are communicated by
the adult, verbally and non-verbally, which help to reassure the child that their
need will be met prior to the actual delivery of food. As we saw in Chapter 3,
adult responses to young children's needs have emotional as well as cognitive

implications, particularly since adults can help young children to 'contain' their feelings through reassuring communication. The child's load can be lightened as the adult communicates their understanding and empathy as well as addressing the child's need. This begins the process of *co-regulation*, in which communicative exchanges occur between adult and child and lay the foundations for *self-regulation*.

Research has shown how caregiver sensitivity in the earliest months predicts better cognitive and emotional outcomes (e.g. Murray, 1992). Such sensitivity entails playful interactions that require effective timing and close attention to a young child's signals, which might reveal, for example, distress from over-stimulation or a need for further attention, so that adults provide a careful balance of stimulation and rest. Studies have also shown how 'emotionally expressive' such interactions are and how such interactions have a cross-cultural 'common dialogue structure' (Underdown, 2007).

Joint attention

Other work, including that of Caplan et al. (1989), has demonstrated how poor attunement can create cognitive and emotional problems – but sensitive attunement also has implications for young children's social development. One of the first signals of social awareness involves the process of establishing what is called *joint attention*. This is essentially a 'state of being' in which two partners (such as a caregiver and child) attend to the same object or event. At around 4 months of age, infants will start to move beyond gazing into an adult's eyes and will start to gaze in the same direction as the adult. This can become a mutual process as adults follow a young child's line of vision and comment on the object or event that is being jointly attended. Research suggests that joint attention plays a fundamental part in early language development and may even predict better linguistic outcomes such as faster vocabulary development (Markus et al., 2000).

Social referencing

Joint attention is closely linked to the process of *social referencing*, which also plays an important part in supporting a child's social, emotional, and cognitive development. When encountering a particular phenomenon, the young child will invariably look to the caregiver for cues on how to respond. The Communicator thus acts as a 'social referee' for the child by role-modelling responses that help to frame young children's understanding and organization of their experiences. The idea of role modelling is supported by Bandura (1977), whose social learning theory highlights how young children imitate those around them. We continue to rely on social referencing from others to help us to know how to behave in social encounters. It also appears to have a particular role to play in the development of empathy (Klinnert et al., 1983). The accumulative effect of communicative processes like joint attention and social referencing help to generate what is known as *inter-subjectivity*.

The development of inter-subjectivity

Inter-subjectivity

Another key aspect of the communicative process is *inter-subjectivity*, which is closely related to attunement (as well as interactional synchrony). It is essentially concerned with developing and co-creating shared understanding (Newson and Newson, 1975). Inter-subjectivity is from the socio-cultural school of thought that emphasizes social interaction and cultural context in the learning process. As with all communication, adults and children use both verbal and non-verbal techniques to generate inter-subjective agreement. The process of inter-subjectivity is not simply about trying to change other people's opinions, like two sides of a debating team. It is about tuning in, sharing experiences, and promoting understanding – it provides a bridge from self to other in order to connect meaning. Trevarthan and Aitken (2001) distinguish between primary and secondary inter-subjectivity. Primary inter-subjectivity essentially entails two-way communication between caregiver and child, whereas secondary inter-subjectivity refers to the inclusion of a third party or object – this process enables young children to realize adults attach meaning to other things.

Inter-subjectivity is not only concerned with communicating personal intentions, it also involves awareness of others' perspectives and thus has important links with the development of empathy. Thus it also has implications for respecting differences as well establishing harmonious relations. Inter-subjectivity is especially important when we encounter children who may not share our own socio-cultural heritage, impelling us to strive for what Fleer (2006) calls 'cultural inter-subjectivity'. This may require adjustment on the part of one or other communicating partner to reach a common interpretation of the meaning that is being exchanged. We may also use inter-subjectivity to assist a child to grasp a particular skill or concept. Some of the ways in which adults promote inter-subjectivity are discussed below and elsewhere (especially Chapter 5).

Child-directed speech

A good example of caregivers adapting their form of communication and connecting effectively is how they appear to adapt naturally the way in which they communicate with young babies and toddlers. Their style of communication changes into simpler, more high-pitched, and exaggerated expressions with clearer pronunciation, slower speech, and repetition of words. This some-times include verbalizing babbling utterances into sentences – in response to a baby babbling 'ba ba ba', the adult might slowly repeat and extend their response using a higher pitch and saying 'Ba ba ba . . . Are you telling me a story? . . . What are you saying? . . . Are you telling me you want this?' This apparently instinctive communicative adaptation is known as *child-directed speech* (formerly called 'motherese' and 'parentese') and it appears that very young children prefer this style of interaction (Cooper and Aslin, 1994). When we employ child-directed speech in our responses to infants and toddlers, we are responding meaningfully and tuning into the child's utterances, inviting interaction from the child. By repeating, elaborating, and exaggerating, our response helps to clarify and often 'upgrade' the child's contribution to the conversation (Pine, 1994). Thus child-directed speech not only involves attunement and helps to generate inter-subjectivity, it also provides a natural *scaffold* for young children's own language development. Providing a supportive scaffold in everyday interactions in explored later in this chapter and more fully in Chapter 5.

The scaffolding process continues as the child matures, as caregivers constantly adjust the length and content of their exchanges, fine-tuning them with increasing complexity. In the same way that experiences of joint atten-tion appear to promote language development, a caregiver's capacity to modify their speech complexity predicts greater language comprehension. Caregiver responsiveness and the capacity to tune into a child's behaviour thus have important implications for language development. Research shows that 'the frequency with which [caregivers] joined in the child's activity, offered verbal prompts, and imitated and expanded on the child's vocalizations predicted how early children attain major language milestones' (Berk, 2003: 366), evidence which no doubt leads Whitehead (2002: 15) to argue that 'all early years settings must be organized primarily around talk and play'. Case Study 4.1 provides an example of this.

Case study 4.1   Effective communication

Helen is an area coordinator for PEEP (Parent Early Education Partnership). It is an early learning intervention that aims to improve the life-chances of children, particularly in disadvantaged areas, by working closely with families through the Learning Together programme. This programme is delivered in a variety of formats and contexts, including early years settings and has a particular focus on supporting young children's language and literacy development and in promoting interaction between parent and child, focusing on communication, responsiveness, and modelling. Research (Evangelou et al., 2005) has shown how parents who participate in the Learning Together programme develop signifi-cantly greater awareness of their child's language and literacy development and ways to foster it, which in turn has a knock-on effect in advancing their children's early literacy skills. The PEEP model is about empowering families to make the most of learning opportunities in the home and to support parents' role as young children's first educators. As a PEEP practitioner, part of Helen's work is to interact with parents and encourage them to become involved with the Learning Together programme, particularly those who are considered 'hard to reach'. She recalls one particular parent with a young baby who had been identified by the health visitor as needing support. Helen visited the parent in her home to try and encourage her to participate in the Learning Together programme that was being implemented during 'Stay and Play' sessions at the local children's centre. Stay and Play sessions provide informal opportunities for parents to bring their babies and toddlers to use the facilities for playful activities and social interaction. To encourage this parent to attend the centre and join in the activities, Helen had to employ all the various attributes and skills discussed in this chapter regarding the communicative act. She knew she had to develop trust and rapport with the parent so that she felt 'safe' and an 'equal'. She had to think about her body language and tone of voice and ensure her message was communicated clearly and sensitively. The parent did come along to one of the sessions and joined in a special group activity initiated by Helen that encouraged parents to share their experiences and to talk about helpful ways of communicating with their babies. During these sessions, Helen had to 'tune into' the parents and hear their voices first in order to build on their natural experiences of communicative exchanges with their child and then assist them in increasing their confidence and under-standing. After participating in the Learning Together programme, the parent said that she had not realized how her baby could benefit from simple activities such as singing or hearing stories at such a young age. She also said that she felt much closer to her baby and was so much more aware of what she thought her baby needed. She communicated much more with her baby and made sure she felt more 'joined in' during whatever she was doing. In effect, she became more attuned to her baby and more aware of how she could assist her child's devel-oping language capabilities.

The Communicator and the communicative act

The communicative act is essentially the exchange of meaning between two humans. It comprises many different elements, both verbal and non-verbal, which form the interdependent parts of communicative behaviour highlighted in this section. One of the earliest forms of the communicative act is the notion of *expressive communication*. This refers to the ways in which infants and toddlers communicate and the various forms this takes, including eye gazing, babbling, and gesturing. Early language development is explored a little more below but in terms of the communicative act, these early forms of communication by very young children have important implications for the adult role. Early exchanges between a young child and caregiver are known as 'protoconversations', in which young children learn one of the most funda-mental 'rules' of the communicative act – *turn-taking*. Research with babies shows how sensitive they are to the structure and timing of interactions from adults and such sensitivity continues as the child ages (Berk, 2003). Turn-taking is still an important part of adult exchanges and it is likely that readers can recall an incident with other adults in which the turn-taking 'rules of engagement' were ignored by an insensitive person.

Paralinguistics

Paralinguistics or non-verbal communication should also be given serious thought by early years practitioners in the communicative act – as much as spoken language – since it is considered that non-verbal communication is at the very least a precursor to children's acquisition and development of verbal or linguistic behaviour (Knott, 1979). Non-verbal communication invariably entails the use of *body language* and Roberts (2002: 8) refers to body language as 'the original language'. Two classic examples of non-verbal communication in young children are 'protodeclarative' and 'protoimperative' gestures, which emerge towards the end of the first year. Protodeclarative gestures involve infants touching, pointing or holding up an object while looking at others to draw their attention to the object/thing the child is focusing on. Protoimperative gestures are similar since they involve pointing or reaching but are used not only to get others to notice the child's interest but to elicit fulfilment of a particular goal, such as reaching up with their arms so that they can be picked up. In both cases, adults' sensitive and proactive responses to these child-initiated gestures play an important part in supporting young children's communication skills and language development.

Elements of paralinguistic communication

While verbal communication increasingly replaces meaningful gestures as the dominant form of communication from the second year of life, paralinguistics continue to play an integral role in the communicative act throughout our lifetime. Non-verbal communication comprises various elements, including *kinesics* – which might involve eye movements, facial expression, posture, and gestures (like the protodeclarative and protoimperative gestures described earlier). Another important way to communicate meaning involves *tactilism* or touching behaviour. The power of gentle touch in facilitating sensitive communication should not be underestimated. *Prosemics* is another dimension not often consciously considered – that is, our perception and use of social and personal space in our efforts to communicate, such as getting down to the child's level thereby decreasing the distance between child and adult. Studies of non-verbal behaviour reveal a complex range of functions whereby non-verbal communication might substitute (waving goodbye), complement (waving while saying goodbye) or support (add more meaning to) the verbal message (waving and crying while saying goodbye).

Kugelmass and Ross-Bernstein (2000) have drawn attention to a number of features involved in the communicative interactions that take place between adult and child in early years settings. They consider many aspects of non-verbal patterns of interactions mentioned above. Their research shows how early years practitioners' use of space and body, such as talking to children at their eye level, smiling or touching them, play an important part in developing attunement and sensitive interactions. We continue to use non-verbal communication as we grow older and it is believed that it accounts for at least 65 per cent of our communication with others (Knott, 1979).

Other strategies within the communicative act that the Communicator can accommodate to maximize effectiveness are the 'pragmatic' elements of communication. As noted in the first section of this chapter, pragmatics is important to ensure sensitive communication, since it takes into account the *context* of the communicative act. Pragmatics helps to govern the nature of the communicative exchange and includes a key conversational skill mentioned earlier – *turn-taking*. Another significant feature is the *use of voice* – specifically how we use it – such as intonation, pitch, speed, and volume, which provide important contextual clues in the communicative exchange. Use of voice is also considered to be a feature of paralinguistics, since a different tone or volume adds another layer of meaning to the spoken words. Use of voice has implications for generating considerate communication, as it can change the whole connotation of the message such as turning a statement into a question. In Chapter 3 we saw how emotion coaching is used to help manage children's behaviour – the use of tone in responding to children's behaviour is of particular importance in adopting emotion coaching techniques rather than more authoritarian approaches.

Another strategy in interpersonal communication is 'shading', an important attribute for caregivers who are aiming to encourage a child to change the direction of their focus by gently modifying the topic of conversation. 'Turnabout', a strategy that is commonly used to foster communication, involves saying something that demands a response from the other conversational partner such as asking a question. 'Shading' might be employed during emotion coaching exchanges while 'turnabout' is an integral feature of what is known as 'sustained shared thinking'. The promotion of sustained shared thinking is a legal requirement for early years practitioners and is part of the EYFS. It is essentially concerned with adult–child interactions that help to support and extend children's thinking and to make connections in their learning. We consider that all the elements of the communicative act discussed in this section, as well as the various attributes applied to the Communicator in this chapter, are necessary for developing effective sustained shared thinking – this is discussed further in the next chapter.

Another pragmatic element of the communicative act is self-evident – the need to communicate clearly. This is known as 'referential communication skills'. Referential communication skills include not only being able to produce clear messages but also being able to comprehend when either your own or another's message has not been properly understood, eliciting the need for further clarification. Referential skills include many of the strategies involved in the communicative act outlined above, both verbal and non-verbal, in helping the Communicator to attune to children and other adults. An early example of a child developing a referential skill is pointing. Referential skills thus help to establish joint attention and inter-subjectivity. The early years practitioner as a Communicator needs to be particularly adept at referential skills to ensure the child or other adults have understood the message coherently. Linked to referential communication skills is 'illocutionary intent', which occurs when the words spoken do not necessarily communicate the speaker's intent. This aspect requires attention on the part of the listener to be aware of hidden, subtle or symbolic meaning and adults need to be conscious of a child's developmental capacity to pick up on such hidden meanings.

Socio-cultural expectations

Illocutionary intent may have socio-cultural associations and is therefore of particular importance for children who may not share the same cultural background as those of the practitioners in an early years setting. This raises an additional pragmatic element to the communicative act – the need to accommodate *socio-cultural expectations*. The adaptations we all make in different social and cultural contexts are known as 'speech registers'. Young children are highly sensitive to such speech registers, as is evident when witnessing young children in role-play enacting different ways of communicating depending on their role, with adjustments made to their tone, use of vocabulary, and body language. An early speech register picked up by infants and toddlers is learning to say 'thank you' (or more often 'ta') as caregivers demand polite forms of exchange. Social expectations in the use of language are invariably loaded with a moral value system that can deliver powerful forms of social and emotional acceptance or non-acceptance in the use of socially and culturally acceptable language practices – what Smith (2004) calls 'the language club'. Attention has been drawn to the way in which adults can act as 'social editors' for young children as they assist in children's 'induction' into social and cultural conventions (Parker-Rees, 2010) and can be related to our earlier discussion of establishing 'cultural inter-subjectivity'.

The art of listening

A final dimension to the communicative act is the art of *listening*. The process of attunement and inter-subjectivity necessarily entails attending carefully to how children are communicating. We will re-visit these ideas in the next chapter, but a good example of how listening to children can be effectively translated into practice comes from early years settings in northern Italy where the notion of listening has been framed into a 'pedagogy of listening'. Their approach has influenced settings in the UK and become popularized as the 'Reggio Emilia approach'. Practitioners who follow the Reggio Emilia approach consider that the main adult role is not so much to 'talk', 'explain' or 'transmit' but *to listen* (Rinaldi, 2005a). Listening is framed in ethical, democratic, and cultural terms rather than as a method – it is about relationships, being part of a community and a sense of belonging. Indeed, a 'pedagogy of listening' incorporates many of the values expressed in the vision of the Communicator being depicted in this chapter – such as sensitivity, openness, and reciprocity – but it also acknowledges that listening involves hearing the many 'languages, symbols and codes we use to express ourselves and communicate, and with which life expresses itself and communicates to those who know how to listen' (Rinaldi, 2005b: 20) – these many acts of communicating meaning are referred to as the '100 languages of children' and relate to our earlier reference to multi-modal communication.

The total communicative act is therefore a combination of elements that the Communicator incorporates into encounters with others to promote more helpful communicative exchanges, as Case Study 4.2 illustrates.

Case study 4.2   Children's voices

Sonia is an experienced early years practitioner who works for the Children's Society supporting early years settings' practices in listening to children's voices. One particular area she has been focusing on is developing helpful ways of eliciting children's views to enhance their participation in the Common Assessment Framework (CAF) process. The CAF is a relatively new form that all professionals working with children in England have to complete whenever they consider children need additional support from other agencies. It is not for cases of child protection, which follow different procedures, but is a communicative tool to help practitioners to understand a child and their family's needs and work together to help fulfil them. It is essentially a shared assessment tool to promote continuity across several agencies. A vital element of the CAF is placing the child and the family at the centre of any work and decisions made; a CAF has to be completed with the child present and incorporates a section asking for the child's views. Sonia has found that engaging with young children while completing a CAF calls for a range of attributes and skills on the part of the adult, not only in helping children feel safe and secure enough to share their views but in helping them to air their views, particularly when they may not be able to use traditional channels of communication. Sonia has developed a number of different strategies that do not always rely on conversation, similar to the Mosaic approach, which is explained in Chapter 6. These strategies provide young children with alternative opportunities for expressing their thoughts, worries, and ideas. Having alternative methods of eliciting children's voices becomes especially crucial when working with very young children who may not be able to express themselves as readily as older children, or with children who find it difficult or traumatic to communicate their feelings and desires through normal communication channels. Sonia knows that listening to children enables us to understand their priorities, what they are interested in, and what concerns them. She also acknowledges that they are experts in their own lives. In one case Sonia worked with an 18-month-old in a nursery to complete the section on the CAF form. The mother was suffering from mental health difficulties and it was identified that extra sessions at nursery would benefit both the daughter and the mother. The girl had minimal verbal language, so the nursery made a book about the girl's day in nursery. They took photos and wrote observations of what she enjoyed, what she disliked, how she was when she arrived, the activities she chose to do, her favourite toys, her friends, the progress she had made, and the next stages to help her development. The child 'spoke' to the practitioners through her activities as they 'listened' to her by paying close attention to what she did. This book enabled the multi-agency panel reviewing the CAF to gain a clearer picture of the girl and it helped them to see the benefits of her attending nursery. In compiling the book, the staff captured the girl's voice and enhanced the information the panel were given through the form. This enabled them to make an informed decision about meeting both the child's and the family's needs.

The Communicator and supporting young children's communicative skills

It is helpful for early years practitioners to be aware of the most effective ways of supporting young children's communicative skills, since this aspect of development has a knock-on effect on many other areas of development. It is not possible in this chapter to provide a full account of what is arguably the most significant and complex aspect of cognitive development in young children. But we are able to portray some of the ways in which we can respond to young children's early communicative abilities more effectively.

Constructivist theory

Many theories have been generated regarding how language develops. Three theorists in particular are mentioned here – Bruner, Piaget, and Vygotsky – because their approaches draw particular attention to how the child engages in the process of learning language. Language development may be a consequence of genetic blueprints and natural physical maturation – a child cannot speak clearly, for example, until the voice box has matured physically to enable full articulation – and it may also be a consequence of our socio-cultural context – how else, for example, do we account for only learning our own native language unless exposed to other languages? Nonetheless, a nature or nurture account of language development may not give sufficient attention to idea that children are proactive participants in their own development. This perspective is emphasized by Piaget, Vygtoksy, and Bruner, who are known as *constructivists*. Each of these key theorists has had a marked influence on how adults interact with children and their ideas are re-visited throughout this book (both the similarities in their perspectives and their differences – for example, how Vygotsky emphasized the socio-cultural context for learning while Piaget concentrated attention on the internal progress of an individual's development). For the Communicator, the important thing to take into account in relation to Constructivism is that children are *active constructors* of their own learning, not simply passive recipients waiting to be reinforced from the outside or genetically programmed from the inside. As supporters of young children's development, we should be aware that children are actively making sense of their world and constructing their own understanding through their interactions with the environment – recognizing this can help us to establish more child-centred practices.

Developmental aspects of language learning

We now know that the process of language development begins from the moment of birth (although some argue that this starts in the womb). Newborns are able to recognize their mother's voice within a few days and begin the process of distinguishing the different phonetic sound units (or phonemes) of their native language so that by 6 months of age they are able to organize speech into the phonemic categories of their own language, and begin to verbalize this via 'cooing' at around 2 months of age using mostly vowel-like sounds ('oo', 'ah') to which repeated strings of consonants are added from around 4 months of age when 'babbling' appears ('babababababa'). Even deaf babies will begin to babble, suggesting a maturational dimension to early speech. With sensitive responses, which might include repeating the sounds back to the baby and employing child-directed speech, babbling vocalizations become increasingly 'speech-like' and it is possible to detect the particular consonant–vowel and intonation patterns of a child's particular language community by 10 months or so. Their phonological awareness expands into larger speech units in the second part of their first year, as they begin to recognize familiar words by being able to detect the speech patterns that formulate common words, eventually leading to vocalization of recognizable words.

In the toddler years (from around 18 months), word learning accelerates, a process known as 'fast-mapping'. Also, word combinations appear (such as 'me up' for 'I want to get up') – known as 'telegraphic speech'. Caregivers can assist these processes through 'recasting' and 'expansion'. *Recasting* entails repeating the child's utterance but restructuring it so that it is grammatically correct, while *expansion* elaborates on the words used by the child (so that a response to 'me up' might be 'I see you want to get up'). By around the age of 6, all the main features for speech and language are in place. As noted above, non-verbal aspects of communication play an integral part in this development of verbal communication but adults' verbalization of young children's gestural communication can support vocalization in language development. We saw earlier how adults might naturally scaffold young children's language development in this way. Bruner (1986), a noted socio-cultural theorist, considers that adults should proactively encourage children to use language to develop their thinking and role-model this in their interactions.

Scaffolding

Research on scaffolding includes the work of Maclure (cited in Barratt-Pugh and Rohl, 2000), who identified four 'types of talk' that adults engage in during interactions with young children: shaping, sharing, supporting, and stretching. For example, by pausing when they communicate with a young child, they *shape* that child's understanding of the 'turn-taking' rule of engagement; by verbalizing what the adult thinks the child is trying to say, the adult is *sharing* the child's perspective and feelings and jointly constructing a shared understanding; by repeating the child's utterances and extending them into fuller sentences, the adult is *supporting* the child's linguistic repertoire; finally, by introducing new vocabulary or by asking open-ended questions, the adult is *stretching* the child. These strategies reflect many of the attributes inherent in the sustained shared thinking exchanges between adult and child in early years settings discussed in the next chapter.

In the scaffolding process, it is important to recognize that *comprehension precedes production* in young children – children are capable of understanding words before they are able to say them. For this reason, many early years settings are increasingly adopting the use of 'baby signing' to support infants' and toddlers' communication. Although its use is controversial, it could be argued that baby signing is simply an extension of a naturally occurring gestural communication (Parker-Rees, 2010). Children also proactively engage in their language learning and 'adopt temporary strategies for producing sounds that bring adult words within their current range of physical and cognitive capabilities' (Berk, 2003: 368). For example, using a single sound to represent a variety of similar sounding words (baba becomes 'baby' and 'bath') or simplifying pronunciation by only vocalizing certain syllables ('banana' becomes 'nana'). These *problem-solving strategies* reflect an inventive mind capable of making proactive adaptations to accommodate physical and cognitive limitations.

Despite such competency, young children are still reliant on others to confer meaning of the words being said, the way in which the words can be structured in a sentence, together with the sounds that they make. Thus, as a Communicator, the early years practitioner needs to pay close attention to the words being emitted by a young child, as this can provide insight into the child's mind and enable adults to tune into the child's interests and views of the world (Whitehead, 2002). In Chapter 6, we will see that children can communicate meaning in many ways other than through speech. Nonetheless, listening to young children's narratives provides insight into their minds, which can help us to secure more child-centred practices and enable us to be respectful of and alert to socio-cultural differences, creating more socially just practices.

The Communicator in adult-initiated and child-initiated activities

As a Communicator, the early years practitioner should employ all the attributes, understanding, and actions outlined in this chapter in their interactions during both adult- and child-initiated activities. If early years practitioners are sentient about the need to tune into the child and promote inter-subjectivity, then the nature and direction of their responses to the child should emerge naturally. If they continue to employ metalinguistic awareness and be alert to the many elements of the communicative act, consciously monitoring their use of body language or tone of voice, this should enhance the quality of the communicative exchange. As with the Carer dimension of the adult role, all aspects of the Communicator role should be considered regardless of whether the activity is initiated by the adult or by the child. At the same time, the very act of communicating with the child will help to inform choices and decisions about whether to initiate activities and when opportune moments for sustained shared thinking might occur. But in all cases, sensitive attunement to the communicative act will help to ensure that all activities ultimately are dependent on the child's needs and interests. As a Communicator, you will be vigilant in listening to the child's 'voice' in all forms and modalities, all the while bearing in mind the possibilities of enhancing the child's development sensitively and collaboratively.

Reflective questions and tasks

1. What kinds of signals and cues would you look for in a young child to help you determine what they are communicating?
2. Observe an adult and child interacting and ascertain which elements of the communicative act are identifiable. Clarify how these elements might have enhanced or inhibited the effectiveness of the communicative exchange.
3. What do you think quality communication should entail?
4. What is your understanding of the term 'cultural inter-subjectivity'?

5 The Facilitator

> Children have to be educated, but they have also to be left to educate themselves.
>
> (Abbé Dimnet)

In this chapter, we focus on the Facilitator self, which emphasizes the reciprocal and responsive relationship between adult and child. In particular, we highlight the adult's role in empowering young children, promoting their autonomy, imagination, decision-making, and problem-solving capacities. In keeping with the book as a whole, we start from the premise that *all* children from birth are powerful, capable, and competent learners, who are eager to learn and connect to others. We know that young children need to be active in their learning – hands on and brains on. Furthermore, play is a key way in which young children experience the world through their interaction with materials, concepts, and people. Significant others also play a vital role in helping young children to make sense of the sometimes bewildering world that surrounds them. Finally, we need to acknowledge children's active role in shaping teaching and learning experiences in the classroom and particularly in their play. We might, then, think in terms of the curriculum and pedagogy as co-constructed: a negotiated space based on a reciprocal relationship between children and the adults who care for and educate them (Rogers, 2010). These principles are underpinned by many decades of robust research and inform the ideas presented in this chapter and the book more generally.

Understanding the term Facilitator

According to established definitions in the literature, 'facilitating' in educational contexts means 'making children's learning easier' (MacNaughton and Williams, 2004), which includes organizing and planning the learning environment and resources. In this chapter, however, we focus on relationships between the adult and child or children, and the strategies adults might employ to facilitate children's learning and well-being. In Chapter 8, we focus more specifically on the practitioner's role in creating a stimulating and supportive space in which children can learn and thrive. In what follows, we try to illustrate why it is important to think in terms of 'facilitating' rather than simply 'teaching', and offer some well-established strategies and frameworks to show how facilitating works in practice together with points for further reflection. Underpinning the idea of the adult as facilitator is the concept of the child as 'active learner', derived from constructivist and socio-cultural theories such as those proposed by Piaget, Vygotsky, and Bruner among others. The ideas stemming from these theorists have had an enormous influence on how adults interact with children in educational settings. We will say more about this later. It is also important to recognize that far from being passive recipients of experiences, young children exercise 'agency' in early years settings, shaping the direction of events and activities. 'Agency' is understood here as a person's way of being, seeing, and responding in the world and taking more control of one's own mental activity but embedded within particular socio-cultural contexts (Edwards, 2001). In the early years setting, children actively respond to and engage with the decisions that are made on their behalf and co-construct curriculum and pedagogy whether we recognize it or not (Rogers, 2010).

As with other chapters in this book, we frame our discussion of the Facilitator of young children's learning firmly within an ethical practice or 'ethic of care' that focuses on 'responsibilities and relationships rather than rules and rights' (Dahlberg and Moss, 2005: 74). In Chapter 1, we endorsed Brooker's (2010: 183) view that caring gives rise to 'ethical politics and to notions of social justice and equality'. Viewed in this way, the Facilitator and Carer share some common ground: without establishing nurturing relationships we are unlikely to capture children's interest in the activities we provide for them or to establish shared meaning, or inter-subjectivity. Nor will we foster a sense of belonging. Within the context of nurturing relationships and an ethics of care, this chapter explores adults' role in scaffolding and supporting learning and development, helping children to create connections and make sense of the world. We consider also an approach to adult involvement that places the emphasis on the reciprocal relationship between adult and child – sustained shared thinking. First, however, a few words on our choice of terminology to clarify our intentions further.

Why 'facilitator?'

The idea of the Facilitator is closely related to how we view pedagogy and the processes of teaching and learning. With this in mind, some readers might ask why we have opted for the term 'facilitator' rather than 'teacher' or 'educator'. We use the term here because it encapsulates a particular way of working with learners (in this case young children), which require professionals to think about an aspect of their work and, we would argue, their professional identity or self, to act in a way that demands a distribution of power and control in the pedagogic relationship. In turn, this pedagogic relationship is nested within the wider context and complex web of interactions in the early years setting, school, family, and community as described by Bronfenbrenner (1979), whose ideas are discussed in more detail in Chapter 6. It is certainly true that the term 'facilitator' has been subject to criticism in educational contexts for its strong association with a particular interpretation of child-centred approaches and a perceived lack of attention to direct teaching, leading some commentators to argue that 'facilitating' requires the adult to adopt a passive role while the child is actively engaged in exploration of and interaction with the environment. Meadows and Cashdan (1988), for example, described the teacher's role within the child-centred model as that of 'guide, friend, counsellor, facilitator', stating that within this model, teacher intervention should be of the gentlest kind. From this perspective, they identify the teacher's main skill in terms of providing appropriate materials for learning, and the structuring of the classroom context, both social and intellectual. 'Standing back', 'watching and waiting' for the child to develop and 'unfold' is one interpretation of this approach.

However, we argue that far from being a passive endeavour, facilitating young children's learning requires high-level interactive skills on the part of the adult. It requires that the adult is tuned into children's thinking and current understanding. Most importantly, it requires adults to *observe* what children do and *listen* carefully to what children say. It requires that adults act ethically, respecting children's emerging ideas about the world, which in turn derive from their particular cultural perspective, the extent and nature of their experiences and specific learning needs. Moreover, the act of facilitating does not preclude direct teaching; facilitators teach and teachers facilitate. We are not, then, rejecting the idea of teaching or teachers in early years settings. However, 'facilitating' young children's learning in such a way that is respectful and meaningful requires considerable knowledge, skill, and understanding on the part of all adults across many different learning contexts. And often it entails being alert to the 'timing' of an intervention – knowing just the right moment 'when a comment, question or suggestion might be useful' (MacNaughton and Williams, 2004: 2). Importantly, it requires that as adults we *reflect* on the power that we hold as more knowledgeable and more mature others, and how this is played out within classroom relationships. We may need at times to relinquish some of the control that we hold so that children have a genuine stake in how things are done and in what may be learned. For some, this will be challenging, particularly if they are subject to external pressures, perceived and real, to meet curricular targets or parental expectations. However, whatever your role, status or qualification, we suggest that acting as a *facilitator* of children's learning is a central aspect of your work as an early years professional. Before we explore some of the ways in which you can facilitate children's learning and development, it is useful to examine some of the dilemmas created for the Facilitator in promoting child-centred practices.

A child-centred pedagogy

The idea of a child-centred pedagogy was introduced in the opening chapter of this book and some of the controversies surrounding what adults ought to do in a child-centred pedagogy were briefly outlined. Differences in theoretical stances towards child-centred education appear to lie in the *degree of freedom* experienced by the child and early years practitioners need to be clear on this issue to understand what being a Facilitator entails, through critical reflection on the different perspectives offered. Wood (2007) has drawn attention to some of the complexities involved in adopting a child-centred pedagogy and the need to clearly examine what the popularized 'slogans' associated with it really mean. She notes that even within one of the main tenets of a child-centred pedagogy – 'meeting children's 'needs' – the notion of 'needs' is not a straightforward matter. Wood poses pertinent questions, such as: Who identifies those needs? How are they identified? How do we meet all these needs? She goes on to say that 'interests' are even more problematic since simply following children's interests is not necessarily practical or even advisable given that such interests might be a 'recipe for anarchy'. Moreover, she claims that 'showing an interest in a range of topics or activities is not the same as making meaningful connections in which learners acquire, test, refine and reflect on their knowledge and skills' (Wood, 2007: 127). Add to this maturational theory and the idea of 'readiness' espoused by Piaget's stages of development, and the implication is that intervention is somewhat pointless until the child reaches a particular age and stage. Bruner and Vygotsky, however, contested Piaget's view and offered a more proactive perspective that suggests how the adult (or peers) within a socio-cultural context can lead children beyond their current capabilities.

Piaget's, Bruner's, and Vygtosky's theories are embedded in child-centred values, such as the idea of the child actively constructing their meaning of the world and yet the adult role manifests itself in different, apparently opposing forms. The Early Years Foundation Stage (EYFS) appears to have resolved this dilemma by accommodating both Piagetian and Vygotskian approaches by advocating both adult-led and child-initiated activities. But we suggested in the Introduction that the terms 'adult-initiated' and 'child-initiated' be used instead, since they co-exist in a process of continuous interaction. As Tzuo (2007: 38) writes, 'teacher control and children's freedom are continually negotiated, engaging in interplay . . . [and] balanced in non-exclusive ways'. Tzuo suggests that a common assumption regarding child-centred education is that it is the opposite of traditional teacher-directed approaches and that the heart of the problem lies with issues of control and freedom, autonomy and authority. This is not necessarily the case. One of the aims of this book is to move away from a dichotomous perspective of child-centred versus teacher-directed to one that envisages young children's development and learning and the role of the adult within it to be driven by fundamental principles that include a child-centred ideology but is able to accommodate elements of more 'directed' acts without necessarily inhibiting children's freedom. As Tzuo (2007: 33) puts it, 'the teacher's role in guiding children's learning is not eliminated in a child-centred curriculum'.

Dewey (1998) is upheld as one of the champions of child-centred education and his work reveals some of the subtleties behind giving children freedom. For example, he considered that child-centred education should be both flexible but firm – flexible enough to allow children to exercise choice but firm enough to allow the teacher to act as an agent of the interests of the group as a whole as well as provide some direction to promote children's individual needs and continuous development. He viewed guidance by teachers as 'an aid to freedom, not a restriction upon it' (Dewey, 1998: 84). Wood also argues that simply allowing children to 'discover everything for themselves, by themselves' is 'enormously frustrating and time consuming' (Wood, 2007: 125). She considers that some aspects of knowledge acquisition lend themselves better to 'discovery learning' than others.

We suggest early years practitioners might reflect on the points presented in this section and relate them to their understanding of and beliefs about child-centred pedagogy in order to envisage how these issues impact on their role.

Listening and participation

The origins of the concept of the facilitator can be traced back to the work of many educationalists, including John Dewey. Carl Rogers developed a helpful framework for understanding the core conditions for facilitating learning, which we have adapted here for the early years context.

Realness in the facilitator of learning or being yourself. To be effective, the Facilitator enters into a relationship with the child without presenting a front or a façade. It means coming into a direct personal encounter with the child, meeting her on a person-to-person basis.

Prizing, acceptance, trust. Prizing the child-as-learner, prizing her feelings, her opinions, her person. Being a Facilitator is caring for the learner and accepting this other individual as a separate person, having worth in her own right.

Empathic understanding. Establishing a climate for self-initiated experiential learning demands empathic understanding. When the practitioner has the ability to understand the child's reactions from the inside, has a sensitive awareness of the way the process of education and learning seems to the child, then the likelihood of significant learning is increased (adapted from Rogers, 1967: 304–11).

These ideas correlate with the 'facilitative qualities' identified by Laevers (1994). These are essentially types or style of adult behaviour and attitudinal qualities that are summarized as a concept of 'engagement'. The first quality encompasses 'sensitivity' on the part of the adult, which entails being attentive, sincere, empathetic, affectionate, and responsive to children's needs and well-being. The next quality identified by Leavers is 'stimulation', which refers to the way in which the adult 'intervenes' in children's activities by suggesting activities, providing information, posing thought-provoking question and other interventions to extend children's thinking, and relates to the notions of scaffolding and sustained shared thinking which are explored later in this chapter. Finally, the facilitative quality of 'giving autonomy' relates to the way in which children are given freedom to experiment, choose and express their ideas and activities, and corresponds to the idea of child-centred approaches.

Being a good listener is at the root of the qualities of the Facilitator suggested by both Rogers and Laevers as well as the strategies of co-construction, scaffolding, and sustained shared thinking discussed later in this chapter. Together with observation, authentic listening shows children that we are interested in them, and that we value their ideas. Global and national initiatives advocate children's active participation and engagement in matters that affect their lives, including legal requirements on the part of professionals working with young children to listen to the 'voice of the child'. The UN Convention of the Rights of the Child (1989) led the way in legitimizing children's right to be heard. In England, the EYFS includes a requirement to listen to children (and carers) and the Childcare Act (2006) places a duty on local authorities to have regard for the views of young children in service provision. As Bath (2009) has shown in her study of reception class children in an English primary school, listening to children is fundamental to inclusive and participatory pedagogy and children's sense of belonging. But what does listening to children actually mean in practice? Lerner et al. suggest six interrelated phases to listening: hearing, focusing on what is heard, identifying what is heard, translating this into meaning, interpreting it, and then remembering it (cited in MacNaughton and Williams, 2004: 115). But listening to very young children demands an approach that takes into account a range of modes of communication. In acknowledgment of the diversity of ways in which young children communicate their needs and interests, Clark and Moss have developed various strategies that adults can use to facilitate the conditions in which young children's voices can be heard. They describe the Mosaic approach as 'a way of listening which acknowledges children and adults as co-constructors of meaning' (Clark and Moss, 2001: 1). The Mosaic approach is a practical means of enabling young children to communicate in a variety of ways using techniques such as cameras and drawings, which enable children's voices to be heard. These are discussed further in Chapter 6. Similarly, Hart (1992) has identified a 'ladder of participation' to alert people working with children to the dangers of tokenistic and paternalistic attitudes towards listening to children. Although Hart's model is associated with children's participation in projects, it can be used as a tool for thinking about the way in which we communicate – not merely listening to children and supporting them to express their views but valuing what they say (Shier, 2001). Hart's model distinguishes between adult-initiated activities where decisions are shared with children and child-initiated activity where decisions are shared with adults. It is child-initiated activity (where children share their decisions with adults) that Hart considers to be the pinnacle of participatory approaches and the 'means by which democracy is built' (Hart, 1992: 5), as well as a fundamental right of citizenship. These points also link to those made in Chapter 3, which highlight how children's treatment by adults and the quality of their interactions pave the way for generating democratic values. In this way, careful listening to and endeavouring to make sense of young children's ideas can help generate mutual understanding, co-ordinated action, and collaborative learning. Bath (2009) and Dahlberg and Moss (2005) also place emphasis on the need for action. How far do we act on what we hear? To what extent do children genuinely participate in the decision-making process in the early years setting? How can we ensure that we act ethically with and on behalf of children in giving them voice? These are very real challenges in the busy early years setting and adults need to reflect carefully on the potential for listening to children to become tokenistic, or to lead to a 'sentimentalism that the pedagogy of listening to children can inspire' (Bath, 2009: 33). Case Study 5.1 illustrates how early years practitioners can facilitate a more genuine pedagogy of listening to children.

Case study 5.1   A pedagogy of listening

Sonia's work with the Children's Society was first illustrated in a case study in Chapter 4. You will recall that the aim of her work is to help to create a culture of children's participation within early years settings. During the last ten years, she has developed a piece of work called the Children's Rights Charter in which settings work towards achieving a certificate to demonstrate that they listen to children and young people. Article 12 of the UN Convention on the Rights of the Child underpins her work and she believes our role as practitioners to is to really listen and tune in to the many different ways children express themselves. She describes below an example of one setting where she was able to support the practitioners to reflect on how they listen to young children and to think about other creative ways to listen and involve children in decision-making.

I worked with a private nursery called Sunflowers in Radstock, which takes children from the age of 2. During the last three years the practitioners have developed how they listen to children and follow their interests. All their planning is based around the children's interests. Encouraged by an article I passed onto them, they have begun to reflect on how they really develop and help the children to think deeply about their interests. When a child/group of children now ask an initial question, rather than rushing onto what else this might lead to, the practitioners have learnt to stop and reflect on that question with the children in more depth. A recent example of this was when a group of children had the thought that dogs liked ice cream. Other children in the group discussed if this was true. As a group, the adults and children decided they needed to find out, so over a few weeks they invited six of their families to bring in their dogs and offer them ice cream. They found five out of the six dogs did like ice cream. They then all decided they needed to write to somebody in their circle of friends, a local vet, to find out what they thought. The local vet wrote back to the children explaining that most dogs did like ice cream, but it wasn't very good for them to eat! She also sent them a book about looking after dogs. During this time the children were finding out about dogs, how to care for them, they were observing dogs, asking investigative questions, and using this information to provide ideas for their play and creative work. The staff have found by allowing the children to ask questions, by investigating with the children together, and by facilitating their opportunities to pursue their interests, they are all extending their learning in unexpected ways.

Socio-cultural perspectives on the Facilitator

We have emphasized the importance of listening to children as a starting point for facilitating learning. Such an approach is located firmly within socio-cultural and critical-social constructivist approaches to children's learning. The important aspect to take into account in relation to constructivist and social constructivist approaches is that children are active constructors of their own learning, not simply passive recipients waiting to be reinforced from the outside or genetically programmed from the inside. Piaget (1970), for example, stated that children do not simply 'copy', they 'act': children are actively making sense of their world and constructing their own understanding through their interactions with the environment. Like Piaget, Vygotsky (1986) also viewed learning as an active meaning-making process but Vygotsky's work built further on that of Piaget by emphasizing the social dimension of learning, with an emphasis on the interaction between the learner and other people. From a socio-cultural perspective, relationships and the interactions that take place within those relationships lie at the heart of pedagogy. In this way, pedagogy means that the adult and the child embark on a learning journey together, where the adult is the facilitator rather than the one who sets a fixed or predetermined path or route. For Vygotsky, the origin of all learning is fundamentally social where meaning is socially constructed during interaction and activity with others and where 'learning awakens a variety of internal development processes that are able to operate only when the child is interacting with people in his environment and in his co-operation with his peers' (Vygotsky, 1978: 104). Thus, for Vygotsky, social interaction plays a central role in learning, especially if the interaction is with more knowledgeable persons: social interaction or cooperation provides the basis for learning allowing further learning to take place. From a Vygotskian approach, when we provide an enabling environment – that is, one which facilitates children's problem-solving – we help them to 'perceive regularities' and 'structures' in the world around them. In effect, pointing out, reminding, suggesting, and praising all serve to structure children's thoughts and activities. Through facilitating this reciprocal way of working, children receive regular affirmative feedback on their efforts, which, according to Cohen (2006), can enhance children's higher-level thinking skills, promote pro-social behaviour, and has the potential to address cultural understanding and social justice in the classroom.

Facilitating learning: Vygotsky's zone of proximal development, metacognition, and 'scaffolding'

Of particular significance to this interactive approach to pedagogy is Vygotsky's notion of the 'zone of proximal development' (ZPD). Put simply, this means that learning depends not only on the state of the child's existing knowledge but also on 'his/her capacity to learn with help' (Wood, 1988: 25); the gap, in terms of 'mental age', between what a learner can do unassisted and what the same learner can achieve with the benefit of a 'more knowledgeable other', which could be an adult or peers. This concept and its practical application have given rise to the idea of *scaffolding* learning, where children are supported by the adult to complete an activity or a task or develop a specific skill in the same way that a scaffold is used to support a building as it is being built or renovated.

Adults might employ a range of strategies to support children, including: modelling and demonstrating; prompting; pointing things out; reminding; suggesting; praising the child's efforts; asking open questions; giving them clues. Such strategies, which we might call 'meta-teaching' (Fisher, 1998), create a supportive framework or 'scaffold' around the child and, according to Vygotsky, assist in the process of structuring the child's thinking and reflective capacities, or metacognitive thinking, which, according to Fisher (1998), is a key element in the transfer of learning. Fisher (1998: 9) describes teaching for metacognition as aiming to 'mediate metacognition to help children make explicit their thinking and learning for the purpose of self-appraisal and self-management'. Scaffolding learning events with children, whether they are adult-initiated or child-initiated, is vital in showing children we are interested in their ideas and in helping them to build confidence in thinking about their thinking. Equally important, however, is recognizing children's need to learn with peers whether in play activities or cooperative adult-initiated tasks.

With babies and very young children, it might be necessary to support their efforts to learn a new skill with playful encouragement and physical support rather than focus on metacognitive strategies. For example, Jesse is 14 months old and learning to walk. As she lets go of the chair that has been supporting her, her key person, Linda, calls Jesse in a playful and encouraging tone, in the spirit of a game, and stretches out her arms to reach her. Jesse shows obvious enjoyment in Linda's playful encouragement and takes a few steps across the room to reach Linda's arms.

Whatever strategies we adopt, working in this way is a shared endeavour, where the child learns that the adult is interested in her and will help her to achieve her objectives, and where the adult learns more about the child-as-learner. In our efforts to support children, we might ask:

- What kind of learner is this child?
- What prior knowledge does this child have?
- What strategies are helpful to this child at this particular moment?

Play as a 'zone of proximal development'

It is worth including in our discussion of the Facilitator some mention of Vygotsky's approach to children's play and especially role-play. His application of the concept of the ZPD in play is very different to that in his broader theory of instruction and learning, which assigned the adult or more knowledgeable other an explicit role in helping children to problem solve and learn new concepts and skills. However, according to Vygotsky, play creates its own unique ZPD, in which children try out a variety of challenging activities and therefore acquire many new skills, learn to self-regulate behaviour, and gain a deeper understanding of situations and roles. This makes play the 'highest level of preschool development'. From this perspective, play is of central importance to the young child's learning and development, not least because it 'continually creates demands on the child to act against immediate impulse' (Vygotsky, 1978: 99). According to Vygotsky, in play, a child is always above his average age, above his daily behaviour; in play, it is as though he were a head taller than himself. For early years practitioners working within a play-based pedagogy, understanding Vygotsky's theory of play may help them to understand why it is important for children to play freely without adult interruptions, especially in situations that allow for children to exercise their imaginations and engage in fantasy/role-play. That is not to say that adults cannot play an active part in fantasy/role-play. It would be difficult to deny that adults have a vital part to play in the provision of and support for children's play experience. Yet at the same time, we need also to recognize children's need to play alone and with friends. There is, after all, a fine line between managing play and facilitating play. Clearly, this is not the case. In relation to the Facilitator, it is important to observe and listen to children and to judge that 'hot moment' when your involvement might help to develop the play, perhaps because it has lost momentum or because the children are struggling to negotiate roles. We argue that the basic principles of facilitation apply equally to adult- and child-initiated activity and that strategies such as scaffolding and sustained shared thinking can be used in both kinds of activity. The type of free play that Vygotsky envisaged will be discussed in more detail in Chapter 7.

Co-construction

Co-construction has come to mean an approach where adults and children mutually construct (co-construct) knowledge and meaning together (Siraj-Blatchford et al., 2002). Jordan (2009) argues that there is a greater possibility of incorporating children's ideas in co-construction than in scaffolding and that as a result it is more empowering for children. A study of children's perspectives of role-play by Rogers and Evans (2008) showed that co-construction is not only a strategy for meaning-making in the context of an activity, but that children can co-construct pedagogy with adults, sharing in the decision-making process in how the environment is organized, and how to approach learning tasks. In particular, Rogers and Evans demonstrated that in the context of role-play, children often adopt strategies to ensure that they can continue to play without interruptions from adults. Rather than create resistance in children, the teachers were able to revise the pedagogic relationship to incorporate children's own perspectives on what would make their play more meaningful. In this way, co-construction has the potential to be applied across a wide range of contexts, thus distinguishing it from meta-teaching and scaffolding, which emphasize extending the child's understanding in the moment or the acquisition of a new concept or skill. Of particular interest to early years practice is Payler's (2009) study of teacher interactions with young children, in which she identified scaffolding and co-construction and the types of inter-subjectivity established between adult and child. Co-construction was more common in preschool settings whereas scaffolding was the preferred approach in the reception classes. To facilitate children's learning and well-being across the early years phase, adults need to consider adopting a range of strategies according to the specific context or activity.

Sustained shared thinking

Several recent studies of early years practice across the world agree that effective pedagogy in the early years promotes scaffolding, co-construction, and the development of metacognition in children (see, for example, Siraj-Blatchford et al., 2002; Jordan, 2009; Payler, 2009). Few would dispute the importance of high-quality interactions for young children's learning, and we would argue also for their general well-being and developing sense of self. A valuable addition to our knowledge and understanding of teaching and learning in early years settings is the concept of 'sustained shared thinking', stemming from the longitudinal EPPE (Effective Provision of Pre-School Education; Sylva et al., 2010) and REPEY (Researching Effective Pedagogy in the Early Years; Siraj-Blatchford et al., 2002) projects. *Sustained shared thinking* offers a useful tool for early years professionals to think about how they can facilitate high-quality interactions in the context of both adult-initiated and child-initiated activities that value the child's interests and abilities while at the same time helping to extend their learning. It is important to emphasize that working in this way is appropriate to both kinds of learning contexts. However, enacting sustained shared thinking in practice is challenging. Part of the skill of the adult is to make conceptual space for the child to contribute his or her ideas by listening carefully to what is said and endeavour to understand what the child means and understands. This is challenging and requires that adults set aside their own ideas, beliefs, and the 'teacherly' desire to give or to get the 'right' answer. Interaction between adults and children and between children lies at the heart of pedagogy. How we interact with children, the teaching strategies we adopt, and the messages we convey in our language and pedagogical approach shape how and what children learn and contribute to how they feel about themselves as learners. The REPEY project defines sustained shared thinking as an episode in which two or more individuals 'work together' in an intellectual way to solve a problem, clarify a concept, and evaluate activities. 'Sustained shared thinking' must contain two key features.

- First, both parties – the adult and the child or children – must contribute to the thinking, although not necessarily equally. The level of contribution will depend upon the nature of the activity and the interaction.

- The second feature is that the ideas put forward and understanding shown must in some way be developed and extended within the interaction.

In England, sustained shared thinking has gained much support as a pedagogical strategy and is included in the statutory curricular framework (the EYFS), particularly in relation to a child's developing creativity and critical thinking, although it is implied in all of the six areas of learning and development. In Learning and Development, under the section on 'Quality improvement', the EYFS suggests that in 'A high quality, continuously improving setting':

- adults are aware of the children's interests and understandings and the adults and children work together to develop an idea or skill;
- in the most effective settings practitioners support and challenge children's thinking by getting involved in the thinking process with them;
- there are positive trusting relationships between adults and children;
- the adults show genuine interest, offer encouragement, clarify ideas and ask open questions which supports and extends children's thinking and helps them to make connections in learning.

(DfES, 2007: 1.28, 9)

Sustained shared thinking, although it might involve talk, is not confined to older children. It is possible to engage in a range of verbal and non-verbal interactions with babies and very young children too. Dowling (2005) provides a helpful framework that can be applied to all age groups:

- *Tuning in*: listening carefully to what is being said, observing body language and what the child is doing.
- *Showing genuine interest*: giving their whole attention to the child, maintaining eye contact, affirming, smiling, nodding.
- *Respecting children's own decisions and choices by inviting children to elaborate*: saying things like 'I really want to know more about this' and listening and engaging in the response.
- *Re-capping*: 'So you think that . . .'.
- *Offering the adult's own experience*: 'I like to listen to music when I cook supper at home'.
- *Clarifying ideas*: 'Right Darren, so you think that this stone will melt if I boil it in water?'

- *Suggesting*: 'You might like to try doing it this way'.
- *Reminding*: 'Don't forget that you said that this stone will melt if I boil it'.
- *Using encouragement to further thinking*: 'You have really thought hard about where to put this door in the palace – where will you put the windows?'
- *Offering an alternative viewpoint*: 'Maybe Goldilocks wasn't naughty when she ate the porridge?'
- *Speculating*: 'Do you think the three bears would have liked Goldilocks to come to live with them as their friend?'
- *Reciprocating*: 'Thank goodness that you were wearing wellington boots when you jumped in those puddles George. Look at my feet, they are soaking wet!'
- *Asking open questions*: 'How did you . . .?' 'Why does this . . .?' 'What happens next?' 'What do you think?' 'I wonder what would happen if . . .?'
- *Modelling thinking*: 'I have to think hard about what I do this evening. I need take my library books back to the library and stop off at the supermarket to get some food for tomorrow, but I just won't have time to do all of these things'.

At the heart of sustained shared thinking is the use of questioning, in particular open-ended questioning, which can extend and develop children's thinking. Questioning is, arguably, the most dominant teaching strategy in classrooms of all age groups. Research has shown consistently that most adult questions are closed (Siraj-Blatchford and Manni, 2008) – they simply require only a 'yes' or 'no' answer. Closed questions as a teaching strategy are limited, since they shut down any possibility for further discussion and extension of ideas. Often, questions asked by adults are designed to elicit the 'right' answer from children and while this is appropriate in some contexts, it leaves little possibility for children to express their ideas and thought processes. Much research has shown that asking open-ended questions can be challenging for practitioners, but open-ended questions lie at the heart of meta-cognition, scaffolding, co-construction, and sustained shared thinking. Case Study 5.2 provides an example of such an approach.

Case study 5.2   Sustained shared thinking

Emma, an early years practitioner who works in a nursery, undertook some action research for her master's dissertation and decided to focus on sustained shared thinking. The following is an extract from her dissertation, which illustrates an episode of sustained shared thinking.

While playing outside the children discovered a kitten (toy) stuck in the guttering of the barn area. The group was allowed time to discover the kitten and talk about how they thought it got there and how it could be rescued.

(P = practitioner)

Child B: Oh, poor kitty, I think she's stuck up there.

Child C: How did it get all the way up there?

P: Oh dear. How do you think the kitten got stuck up there in the first place?

Child A: He climbed up this pipe (pointing to the drain pipe), then went along here and got stuck in here.

Child C: He can't climb up there 'cos' he's not real! I think he must have been 'throwded' up there.

P: Who do you think might have done that?

Child C: I don't know but it's not very kind is it? They might have done it on accident.

Child A: Yeah, like this (he mimics throwing an imaginary object accidentally!)

Child E: My daddy 'throwed' the ball through the window by accident. Mummy was cross. He 'breaked' the window!

P: Yes, they might have done it by accident, I can't think that anyone would throw it up there on purpose. Well, I suppose we need to do some good thinking about what to do to help the kitten. How shall we do that do you think?

Child D: I know, I know! We can, we can ask Charlotte to climb up all the way.

Child A: Yeah, I seen Charlotte climb ladders to get that stuff off them tall shelves in the other room.

Child C: Or we can get Jill to do the ladder.

Child B: No, she don't really like 'um' (meaning ladders).

Child C: I know, we can find Graham, he's good with ladders and he fixes stuff.

Child E: Yeah, ask Graham to do it.

P: What do we need to ask Graham?

Child E: Ask him to get the ladders and climb up there.

P: Oh I see.

Child D: He can climb all the way up to that pipe thing and put it (the kitten) in his pocket.

Child B: He 'don't' want to squash it though. That would hurt it, wouldn't it?

Child A: Poor kitty. I think he's very sad. I don't want him to be sad no more.

Child E: No.

P: Shall we decide what we think we should do then?

Group: Yeah!

P: Well, you had lots of thoughts and ideas, let's see if we can choose one idea to sort the problem out. You said we need to get a ladder but who shall we ask to climb up it, you thought it could be Jill, Graham or Charlotte. Who do you think would be best to ask?

Child C: Graham.

Child A and E: Yeah, we can ask Graham.

P: What makes you think Graham will be best for the job of getting the kitten down?

Child E: He can climb ladders up really high.

Child D: Yeah, I 'seen' him before on ladders. He can put it (kitten) in his pocket gently, can't he?

Child B: He mustn't drop her or she'll have a headache and she might die!

P: I hope she doesn't do that! Okay, so you think Graham can climb the ladder and put the kitten in his pocket gently and bring it back down again?

Child A: Yeah, really gentle!

Child B: And then the kitten will live happily ever after!

(Bowery, 2008)

The Facilitator in adult-initiated and child-initiated activities

The Facilitator embraces a central notion proposed by this book: that rather than thinking in terms of adults *directing* children's learning, activities in early years settings may be *initiated* either by the adult *or* by the children but then can become a shared endeavour – a process of co-construction and negotiation within a reciprocal and responsive relationship. We have emphasized also that the Carer and Communicator dimensions of the adult role are integral to the effective functioning of the Facilitator self and to developing a dialogic approach to teaching and learning, an idea contained within the concept of 'scaffolding' and more recently, 'sustained shared thinking' with children. Early years practitioners will draw on a range of strategies and skills to *facilitate* young children's learning and development during their everyday activities, such as sensitively tuning into children's needs and interests, being alert to finding the 'right moment' to interact and considering what kind of interaction might be appropriate – modelling, commenting, asking open questions and/or making suggestions. Such an approach will of course include creating adult-initiated opportunities for extending children's thinking and learning, but always with the intention of empowering young children to be active agents with the Facilitator acting as a 'guide by their side'.

Reflective questions and tasks

1. What does authentic listening to young children involve?
2. How will you distinguish between 'scaffolding', 'co-construction', and sustained shared thinking'?
3. How would you describe your role as a facilitator?
4. Observe and give feedback to a colleague engaging in 'sustained shared thinking'. How might this process differ between a toddler and a 4-year-old?

6   The Observer

All ideas come about through some sort of observation.

(Graham Chapman)

This chapter and the two that follow form the trilogy of the Observation, Assessment, Planning (OAP) cycle that is embedded in the everyday practice of all early years settings. We consider why observing children is important and cover a range of purposes for undertaking observations, including the need to identify children's needs, interests, and achievements and ensure the quality of the provision. We look in particular at observing children's symbolic representations and its importance in the development of children's thinking. In doing so, symbolic representation is explained and suggestions made with regard to the way in which early years practitioners can be alert to its development in young children. We suggest that early years practitioners need to have a very clear rationale for undertaking planned observations to ensure that they are valid, purposeful, and ethical.

The observing professional

Statutory obligations

In England, the Early Years Foundation Stage (EYFS) firmly endorses the OAP cycle by including the requirement that practitioners provide 'ongoing observational assessment to inform planning' (DfES, 2007: 1.18) incorporating an Observation, Assessment, Planning commitment within the 'Enabling Environments' theme. The EYFS also states that 'all planning starts with observing children in order to understand and consider their current interests, development and learning' (DfES, 2007: 3.1). Practical guidance is offered to practitioners to help them to know what to look out for in the 'look, listen, and note' sections of the non-statutory parts of the EYFS and to link these to the early learning goals to increase their knowledge of the child and to plan for appropriate provision.

Moreover, according to the EYPS Standards, to generate effective practice, early years professionals need to 'use close, informed observation and other strategies to monitor children's activity, development and progress systematically and carefully, and use this information to inform, plan and improve practice and provision' (S10). Interestingly, the QTS Standards do not specify any need for practitioners to observe children, although this requirement is implicit in the Standards that expect teachers to assess and monitor children's progress (Q12, Q26). The statutory requirement for reception teachers to formally assess children's progress against thirteen assessment scales derived from the Early Learning Goals of the EYFS stipulates that such assessments should be based on the ongoing observations of consistent and independent behaviour undertaken largely in the context of children's self-initiated activities. We will look in more detail at the Foundation Stage Profile in the next chapter but the main point to note here is that observation *triggers* the OAP cycle, acting as a precursor for the fulfilment of many other aspects of the EYFS, QTS and EYPS Standards in England.

Understanding the term 'observation'

The term 'observe' literally means to 'see and notice' or to 'watch carefully'. Observation has been described as 'getting close to children's minds and feelings' (Drummond: 1998: 105). It enhances our understanding of children and their actions and enables us to take responsibility for helping a child to progress. Importantly, observations provide us with information and evidence about young children's needs, interests, and achievements, which helps us to build up child-centred provision.

The purposes of observation

There are two practical purposes to conducting observations. The first is to provide information on children's needs, interests, and achievements that can be fed into the cycle of assessment and planning phases and inform the creation of an appropriate learning environment. Part of this process entails sharing observations with caregivers and it thus becomes an important channel of communication for children's families (Palaiologou, 2008). The second main purpose behind observation is to enable practitioners to gather evidence in order to evaluate their own practice and make necessary adjustments and improvements. We saw in the Chapter 2 how action research is one possible way to ensure critically reflective provision and that undertaking observations is a powerful tool for systematic investigation of a particular aspect of practice.

Being an Observer can therefore help us to be more competent and 'tuned in' to the children in our setting. Our everyday, 'on the hoof' observations will also assist in this process as we learn from what children say and do and connect these insights with the academic and intuitive theories we hold. Linking theory to practice in this way can provide a basis from which to challenge existing orthodoxies about children's learning and development that may not be appropriate, as Chapter 2 demonstrated.

Broadening the vision behind the purpose of observations

While observations help us to fulfil our professional legal obligations and to improve practice, we suggest a broader vision of the purposes of observation, that as an Observer you can be fundamentally guided by the *child-centred and socially just* pedagogical practices that were outlined in the Introduction and in the preceding chapters. Taking this view is necessary so that the statutory requirement to use observation to help children to make progress towards the early learning goals does not dominate observational practice and therefore obscure and exclude the difficult to measure and less predictable aspects of children's learning. This is not to say that 'tick box' observations do not have a place in the Observer's repertoire, but we need to be wary of only envisaging the purposes of observation in terms of checking children's achievements. We must remember that the statutory framework of the EYFS also compels practitioners to observe children's *needs and interests* and, as part of this process, to ensure *equality of opportunity*. Therefore, the *ultimate purpose* of observations is to ensure child-centred and socially just practice. So how is this broader vision manifested in observational practices?

Child-centred observations

In child-centred observations, the starting point is the child and what children *can* do rather than what they cannot do – in other words, we have a *presumption of competence* about the child. By envisaging the child as competent and capable, practitioners can look forward and help them to build upon their current capabilities rather than judging them from a deficit perspective. Observation works best when children are engaged in child-initiated playful activities because this is when children exhibit their authentic needs, interests, and achievements, and when practitioners can build a rounded picture of a child's social, language, and physical skills as well as their application of knowledge and understanding about the world.

Socially just observations

Socially just observations entail being mindful of *why* we are conducting an observation. By having a clear rationale for the observation, practitioners can ensure the observation has *validity* and that it is undertaken in an *ethical manner.* An Observer will be respectful and cognisant of the power they hold in conducting observations of young children and the accompanying judgements that are made about them. As Willan (2010: 67) notes, 'observing children is not a neutral process'. The ethical issues involved in observing children are considered further in Chapter 7, where we examine how our values, beliefs, and expectations – our professional knowledge – relating to young children fundamentally influence the assessments we make in our evaluations of the observations made. When observing young children, it is important to adopt an *ethic of care* and follow *ethical protocols* such as taking into account issues of *confidentiality*. We need to pay particular attention to the subtleties of the communicative process such as body language and recognize that young children communicate their needs, interests, and achievements in many different ways, as we will see later in this chapter. Socially just observations also help to focus attention on whether provision is *inclusive* and *anti-discriminatory*.

The importance of context

Observation is a 'dynamic undertaking conducted within a context of continuous change' (Willan, 2010: 63), and we need to envisage ourselves as evolving practitioners ready to accommodate the rapid change that occurs both in our daily practice and more generally in the world. But at a more immediate level, we need to remember how *context* shapes what can be known about a child and what we will see. Children need to be observed in different contexts and situations to gain a fairer and more holistic perspective of their capabilities, and alternative perspectives sought, including the child's – in other words, through the different 'lenses' that were suggested in Chapter 2. Indeed, the statutory requirements of the EYFS require that observational evidence is drawn from a 'wide range of learning and teaching contexts' (DfES, 2007: 2.19). We also need to take into account other *contextual factors* such as how the child is positioned in relation to gender, cultural identity or social class and, in turn, how these might affect the nature of the observation and its evaluation.

Child-centred observations

Selecting appropriate methods

We saw in Chapter 5 the need to adopt child-centred practices, which include viewing the child as intrinsically curious and capable, respecting children's needs and interests, and being committed to active learning and play. Such a vision can be extended to the way in which we conduct observations. From a pragmatic perspective, our observations need to be manageable and feasible but their manner and form will be driven by the need to capture the authentic 'voice of the child'. This 'voice' will be an expression of their needs, interests, and achievements but the format or formats used to collect this information may change depending on the focus, just as the format we choose will influence the information gathered. It is important to remember that whatever observational approach is used, it must be *fit for purpose* – that is, the observational tool chosen is relevant, valid, and effective for the observational purpose.

Participatory methods

There are a number of well-established observational methods documented in the literature, including participant observation, 'on the spot' observation, and non-participant observation. In brief, *participant observation* occurs when a practitioner is *in situ* and working directly alongside children during an interaction or activity. It is unstructured and narrative and notes relevant information about the child's needs, interests, and/or achievements. *On the spot observations* can occur at any time when a practitioner notices something about a child that is pertinent, and a common approach is to write these on Post-it® notes. *Non-participant observations* are invariably pre-planned, often have a predetermined aim, and entail a range of different techniques, including 'target-child' observations, which track a particular child, and 'time or event sampling', which record particular incidents or note particular information at timed intervals. Or it could involve some kind of formal measurement, such as checking a child's achievements against the early learning goals. All of the observational formats mentioned in this section might also be used to evaluate provision as a whole as part of an action research study.

However, our interest in this chapter is to foreground *participatory* observational approaches to ensure that observational practice fully captures the 'child's voice'. Participatory methods need to be distinguished from the participant and non-participant observations described in the previous paragraph – they are not participant methods, they are *participatory*. These methods directly elicit the 'child's voice' by involving the child (and their caregivers) in the observational process. Participatory techniques assume a child's competence and expertise in their own lives, and are flexible, creative, non-threatening, and context-appropriate. Clark and Moss (2001) have developed the Mosaic approach as a means to enable children to actively contribute to the OAP cycle. The emphasis is on using developmentally appropriate techniques that enable young children to express themselves and the way they perceive the world more freely and on their own terms.

The Mosaic approach

The methods suggested by the Mosaic approach provide practitioners with opportunities to listen to children's perspectives on their lives. It is in the

Mosaic approach that we can see a broader interpretation of the term observation and of being an Observer – here the observations help to create what Clark and Moss (2001) call a 'climate of listening', which goes beyond the traditional techniques carried out by adults mentioned earlier. A range of participatory tools is used, including the use of cameras by children, which provides a user-friendly means of prompting young children, particularly those with less well-developed verbal communication skills, to express their views about, for example, aspects of the provision that they consider to be of interest or of importance to them. Case Study 6.1 provides some examples of different participatory techniques.

Case study 6.1   A Mosaic approach

Kim works in a nursery attached to a primary school and has just completed her EYPS validation. She was given the responsibility of developing the outdoor area because this had received a poor evaluation in a recent Ofsted inspection. She considered what had been said about the outdoor area by the inspection team and also revisited the EYFS and the requirements for outdoor provision. She also discussed the matter with the rest of the staff and ascertained their views on how the outdoor area could be developed. But she felt that it was important not only to include the children's perspectives but to actively engage them in improving their outdoor experiences as partners in the process. During her studies she had come across the Mosaic approach and some research that had been done on children's 'spaces to play' (Clark and Moss, 2005) and decided to use this as a means to compile a collection of observational material on which to base any decisions made about changing the outdoor area.

Kim started by giving children some disposable cameras and asked them to photograph their favourite places and activities in the outdoor area. The photos were collected together into a photobook and she used these visual images to develop a 'child-conference' discussion with the children about the outdoor area – about things that were good and to get new ideas. She also went on walking tours of the outdoor area with the children, talking to them about the area, which was recorded on video. She also decided to include some out-of-setting visits with the children to outdoor play areas in the community and this was done in the spirit of a 'walking tour' to stimulate further discussion. The children also took the photographs they had taken home to share with their families, and caregivers were invited to write their own comments about their children's experiences of outdoor activities in the home or elsewhere to add to the information and asked their views about their children's needs, interests, and achievements in outdoor learning. Kim also asked the children to create plans of the outdoor area and drawings of different activities and resources that could be used. Sometimes this meant becoming involved in animated discussions about various issues, such as the feasibility of some of the ideas suggested (e.g. the children came to recognize that time and space would not permit a hammock swung between two large trees), or together attempting to resolve a problem, such as getting hold of various materials to make dens that the setting did not have. Kim felt that these sorts of discussions were of particular value, as they enabled her and the children to engage in many 'sustained shared thinking' moments.

On the basis of the children's contributions, caregivers were invited to contribute resources as well their own ideas. A display was created of all the observational material collected and caregivers were invited to share their thoughts about developing the outdoor provision. All the different perspectives were discussed at staff meetings as well. The ongoing collection of observational material and the shared reflections and decision-making made on the basis of this evidence eventually led to the creation of a vibrant and stimulating outdoor environment that contained a whole range of new resources and opportunities for playful activities. When Kim went back to the statutory information, she realized that all the criteria for outdoor provision had been met but it had come from the children as collaborators and co-researchers.

The Mosaic approach gathers a range of material together to build up a child's portfolio and to create a profile, each piece contributing to the 'mosaic'. Thus the term 'mosaic' reflects the different pieces of evidence that are collated together to provide an overall picture of children's perspectives of their world alongside the views of the adults who care for them. The Mosaic approach also endorses the EYFS requirement of parental partnership and ongoing dialogue in the OAP process.

Learning journeys

We saw earlier how important it is for the Observer to ensure that their observations are purposeful and to clarify *why* the observation is taking place. How much we record or document is another dimension to consider. Katz and Chard (1996: 3) comment that documentation need only occur when 'children are engaged in absorbing, complex, interesting projects worthy of documentation'. As the Mosaic approach shows, documentation comes in many forms, including traditional written observations as well as media-based formats – photographs of children's work, audio and video recordings. Indeed, digital technological advances have revolutionized the way in which young children's learning can be documented. If practitioners are to record this evidence, a key question to keep in mind is: Who is the audience for all this recorded work?

Documentation should only be undertaken if it has a clear *purpose* and reflects the dynamic nature of the OAP system, with each aspect of the cycle informing the others. One possible approach, common in early years settings in England, is to create *learning journeys*. Learning journeys are observational narratives or stories about a child's learning that can be depicted in various formats, not just written observations, and typically describe a particular learning sequence or activity undertaken by a child linked to the early learning goals and/or highlight a particular achievement or interest, and contain a 'next steps' section which suggests a possible future activity. Learning journeys can be expanded into a portfolio of various different pieces of information from a range of observational formats (written observations, assessments of early learning goals, 'next steps' plans, photographs, children's drawings), which collectively portray a child's learning and development. Learning journeys are based on the Te Whāriki model of 'learning stories' devised in New Zealand (New Zealand Ministry of Education, 1996).

The use of 'learning stories' reflects the principles and values of Te Whāriki, which emphasizes child-centred and inclusive practices particularly in relation to cultural identities, as well as children's freedom and ownership. Te Whāriki centres on empowering and valuing young children and ensuring that their interests and aspirations are met. Narrative observations are made on the basis of identifying children's needs and interests and practitioners use this information to formulate 'learning stories' about the children. So learning stories are essentially 'a method of documenting everyday interactions' and contain 'snapshots' or 'vignettes' of children's learning (Carr et al., 2005: 141). They are a 'window on the meaning that children are constructing' (Carr, 2001: 181). Learning stories are always shared with both the children and parents, alongside discussion and decision-making among the children and staff to plan, enrich, and progress children's learning – photographs are often taken to help young children 'read' their learning stories, since they provide a 'visual language' (Clark and Moss, 2001). It is collaborative and community-based and reflects the learner's personal development rather than performance indicators – in other words, it is *participatory*.

Although the learning journeys used in early years settings in England may not replicate the learning stories of the Te Whāriki model, it is helpful to incorporate the key principles underpinning the approach taken in New Zealand given their child-centred nature. If learning journeys are to be used as the main documentary evidence of children's learning and progress, care needs to be taken to ensure a system is developed that enables practitioners to transfer the observational evidence into the learning journey, incorporate an assessment of the observation, and feed this evaluation into the planning of provision (or creation of provision as we prefer to call it). This leads us to consider another key question: what should these learning journeys contain?

Tracking significant moments

Hutchin (2003) has suggested that observations should be about tracking *significant achievements or moments* – that is, noticing particular accomplishments such as attempting something that has not been tried before, applying a new skill in a different context, expressing something new, persevering in an activity or collaborating with others for a long period. These significant moments can be recorded and incorporated into the child's learning journey portfolio and subsequently fed into the rest of the setting's OAP system. (The case study in Chapter 7 provides an effective example of how one setting has successfully incorporated learning journeys into their OAP system.) Significant moments might include observing a baby's preoccupation with a particular object, witnessing a toddler climbing a ladder or noting a young child's cooperative play with a peer in building a block tower. Significant moments thus encompass a wide spectrum of children's experiences – but it is helpful to gain a clearer insight into young children's thinking in order to help understand what a child's significant moments might be. The remainder of this chapter therefore reviews the notion of *symbolic representation*, which will help practitioners to ascertain the significant moments of young children's learning and development.

Observing symbolic representation

A central focus for the Observer is likely to be observing young children's development of *symbolic representation* and this section clarifies what this entails. Understanding and recording the processes of symbolic representation are of particular importance given the insights they can provide into young children's thoughts, feelings, and actions. Like most terms, symbolic representation is not easy to define but it essentially entails the way in which we make sense of external reality by representing our experiences internally – experience is actively organized into internal mental or cognitive structures called 'schemes'. Although it is largely a cognitive process in which an external entity comes to stand for or be represented by a mental or cognitive symbol or image, the socio-cultural influences on this internal psychological process must always be acknowledged. First, it is helpful to know about some of the key theory that has been generated regarding symbolic representation.

Theories of symbolic representation

A number of attempts have been made to theorize the process of symbolic representation as a way of understanding children's cognitive development, most notably by Piaget (1978) and Bruner (1990). For Piaget, children make sense of the external world by internally constructing and representing know-ledge in the form of 'schemes' (also known as 'schemas'). Schemes are essen-tially cognitive forms of organized thought that enable us to code our perceptions and understanding in meaningful ways. They are dynamic struc-tures or 'working theories' that are constantly changing as the child engages with the world. Piaget identified two processes that help to explain how chil-dren's thinking becomes more complex: *assimilation* and *accommodation*. Assimilation occurs when new experiences are easily interpreted, as they 'fit' into or match existing schemes or working theory, whereas accommodation occurs when changes need to be made to the existing scheme or working theory to incorporate new insights so that a restructuring of the scheme occurs.

The representation of knowledge is thus an active process and children constantly *adapt* their schemes to make sense of new experiences and devise new working theories. Thus external actions/events/objects are turned into schemes, which may take the form of images or symbols that enable us to repre-sent the world and make sense of it. As mentioned previously, this process is one of active construction, since the child is re-presenting the experience (hence the term Constructivist – see Chapter 4). According to Whitehead (2002: 58), these representations or schemes 'allow us to select, hold on to, understand and share our emotionally, intellectually and culturally meaningful ideas'. In other words, complex thinking evolves via symbolic representation.

Piaget viewed symbolic representation as developing through a series of universal, pre-ordained stages. The first two stages are the most pertinent for early years practitioners: the *sensori-motor* and the *pre-operational* stages. Babies begin to actively construct schemes through their sensory and physical activ-ities, which initially begin as 'chance behaviours' (Berk, 2003) motivated by their basic needs and exploratory drive. For example, a 'dropping scheme' develops as a baby grasps and releases an object by accident, which then evolves into a more sophisticated, self-controlled, and deliberate 'dropping scheme' through constant practice. According to Piaget, by the age of 2 toddlers are able to mentally represent the world as images or concepts and are less reliant on the concrete physical world to manipulate their own thinking. Images in the mind build on and extend the earliest 'action' representations and culminate in more logical and cultural classifications, notably language.

However, one of the main criticisms of Piaget is his emphasis on the maturational dimension to cognitive development and his categorization of symbolic representation into age-related stages. Although it is true that some elements of physical maturation need to occur before a child is capable of performing certain actions, subsequent work has shown that Piaget may have underestimated young children's capacity to think and ability to represent the world symbolically (see, for example, Donaldson, 1978). More emphasis is now given to the impact of the socio-cultural context on children's learning and development, such as in the work of Bruner.

Bruner's (1990) contribution to our understanding of symbolic representation moves away from a maturational, stage-dependent perception of cognitive development. He also identified different forms of symbolic representation that reflect Piaget's stages of cognitive development, but he did not tie these into a particular maturational age – he called them 'modes of representation' rather than stages, since they are integrated and only loosely sequential. He considered that both adults and children can experience the three dimensions or 'modes' of representation at any age: the enactive, the iconic, and the symbolic. When adults or children are in the *enactive mode*, they represent the world through motor responses or actions; in other words, knowledge is stored primarily in the form of sensori-motor responses (and closely resembles Piaget's sensori-motor stage) – in the enactive mode, knowledge can only be understood or expressed through actions. In the *iconic mode*, we represent the world via images or pictures; in other words, knowledge is stored primarily in the form of visual images – pictures or images are needed to understand or express knowledge. Finally, in the *symbolic mode*, we are able to represent the world symbolically in a variety of forms that are free from the immediate context and are not reliant on visual images (similar to Piaget's pre-operational stage); in other words, knowledge is stored primarily as words, mathematical symbols or via other symbol systems – we can understand or express our knowledge using words or other symbols. Language is possibly the most important and powerful symbolic system and we have seen some of the ways this develops in the Chapter 4. Bruner considered that children think through these modes because actions, images, and words are *used by people around them and in their interactions with them*.

So how can we recognize children's modes of representation? The remainder of this section offers some helpful ways in which we can observe the symbolic representational processes of young children.

Schema theory

Athey (2007) attempted to apply Piaget's notion of schemes to early years practice and developed the notion of schema theory (or scheme theory). Her work was based on her observations of babies and toddlers and she noticed the repeating patterns of behaviour in young children's play, which led to the identification of a series of schemas that young children experience. Athey translated Piaget's notion of schema to be a 'pattern of repeatable actions that lead to early categories and then to logical classifications' (Athey, 2007: 48). Such patterns of behaviour reflect how young children's experiences are assimilated and gradually coordinated. The need for young children to repeat behaviour is understandable from a neurological perspective, since connections between nerve cells need to be constantly reinforced or the connections will be lost. This process is known as *synaptogenesis* and involves the pruning of synaptic connections between nerve cells depending on whether they are sufficiently stimulated. This highlights the importance of repetition and explains why babies and toddlers are driven to keep dropping objects again and again or to hear the same nursery rhyme over and over. The development of schemas in babies and toddlers is based on the senses and on movement and action (sensori-motor). For example, in babies the schemas of 'tracking and gazing' reflect one of the first great cognitive 'accommodations' as babies learn that objects can be stationary or can move.

As children grow older and expand upon their experiences, they engage in a range of symbolic behaviours. Bruce (2010) offers the example of 2-year-old Danny who often plays with toy cars and uses a cardboard box as a garage. He pushes the cars up the sides and into the corners of the box. He also plays with boats and pushes them under the water around the water tray and into every part of the water tray. Danny is developing his 'containing' schema and through this schema he is developing concepts of perimeter, angle, vertex, cube, cuboid, edge, inside, and so on. A child sliding down a slide may be experiencing the 'transporting' schema but is also learning about motion, gravity, forces, friction, velocity, and momentum. By observing these patterns of behaviour and symbolic play activities, the Observer can feed this information into the next stage of the OAP cycle in order to build on these developing interests by providing a range of interesting and stimulating experiences which extend thinking along similar lines.

Emotional and social schemas

Schemas do not only reflect developing scientific or mathematical concepts, since young children also formulate functional emotional and social schemas or templates that reflect how we represent our relationships with the world and our own sense of self. Emotional and social schemas help to determine and regulate interpersonal relationships – the *internal working model* of relationships described in Chapter 3. Arnold and practitioners at the Pen Green Children's Centre have researched young children's emotional schemas and have shown how young children 'seem to use schemas or repeated patterns of action for comfort, to give form to, and to explore and begin to understand complex life events and changes' (Arnold et al., 2010: 11). They suggest that young children may use schematic behaviour to help them to understand and come to terms with emotional events such as separation and loss. For example, they illustrate how some children might use the 'transporting' schema by transporting objects from home to nursery to provide them with a sense of security. Arnold et al. relate this phenomenon to Winnicott's work, who called such objects 'transitional objects' representing comfort and security in helping to alleviate young children's anxiety. Such emotional and social representations serve to illustrate how schema development is both a cognitive and affective process and can reveal young children's emotional and social worlds, including revealing underlying emotional issues. Arnold et al. (2010) also contend that manifestations of young children's emotional and social representations through their symbolic schematic behaviour also reveal their engagement with moral issues.

Multi-modal representation

Other evidence of young children's developing symbolic representation comes from observing *multi-modal* activities. We referred to young children's multi-modal ways of communicating through verbal and non-verbal interactions in Chapter 4 and Worthington (2007) has also highlighted how multi-modal ways of representation help children to explore symbols – their meaning and their interpretation. Multi-modal representation refers to the multiple and diverse ways in which children *make meaning* through the use of different resources or tools and is expressed in many different forms.

Kress (2000) suggests that long before children are able to read and write in the adult sense, they are able to express their views, thoughts, and identities in a variety of ways to demonstrate what they mean. Multi-modality is essentially the way in which 'texts' and meanings are made, represented, communicated, and understood by individuals within social contexts. Such 'texts' include visual images, gesture, speech, sound, movement, spatial and print-based texts. Multi-modal 'texts' show how children understand the world and what they are interested in. Children can imitate and re-create their experiences via role-play, oral narratives, model-making, drawings, and other mark-making activities, musical and dance activities, and so on. The potential for children to generate such 'texts' is reflected in the words of Malaguzzi (Rinaldi, 2005a), who referred to children's capacity to represent their world symbolically in a variety of ways as 'the 100 languages of children'.

We also saw earlier how schemas have been described as 'working theories'. Te Whāriki refers to the 'more elaborative and useful working theories' that children develop about 'themselves, people, place and things in their lives' (New Zealand Ministry of Education, 1996). It is possible to discern these working theories in action through their expression in multi-modal representational activities that help children to make sense of their world, give control over what happens, for problem solving and for further learning (Carr, 2001).

Representational activities

Mark-making is a common form of multi-modal activity in young children. Matthews (1999) notes that children's early mark-making, which often appears as mere 'scribbles', is actually the product of a 'systematic investigation rather than haphazard actions'. Young children's initial mark-making reflects their early physical movements or actions and their visual representation of the world evolves alongside their physical development. Formal writing emerges from the gradual configuration of patterns and lines into differentiated marks and recognizable, conventional symbols. Writing and reading, like talking, mark-making, and symbolic play (such as role-play), should not be viewed as separate developments, although they have their own special aspects. In creating opportunities for children to make multiple associations between, for example, talking, drawing, and writing, they can build up an understanding of the differences and links between symbols and signs and how they encode meaning. Reading is as much about the development of this understanding and of meaning-making as it is to do with recognizing shapes, chanting sounds, and scanning lines of print.

Similarly, a government review of mathematics (DCSF, 2008b) has emphasized the importance of valuing and supporting children's mathematical 'marks' or graphics to support their mathematical thinking and processes. Often children are not encouraged to represent their mathematical thinking unless standardized symbols are used, such as $1 + 1 = 2$. Carruthers and Worthington (2006) have shown how children's early mathematical graphics or marks support their mathematical thinking as they explore the symbolic language of maths. Thus, informal mathematical mark-making is an important stage in developing children's formalized understanding of standardized maths. Graphics include tally-type marks and invented numerical symbols which lay foundations for later standard written forms and abstract thinking. According to Carruthers and Worthington (2006), we need to view children's mathematical mark-making not in terms of 'human sense' but in terms of 'child-sense' to understand their thinking, and this idea applies equally to all multi-modal activities.

Whatever the medium of representation, children's representation of the world is often accompanied by a verbalized story commentary. Kress (2000) argues that the interpretation of the end product, such as a drawing, may not provide sufficient information or understanding about the intent or meaning the child is trying to convey. If an Observer pays as much attention to the oral commentary that accompanies older children's representational activities as the product, they can often gain a clearer understanding of the children's intentions. It also opens up opportunities for practitioners to engage in collaborative dialogue with young children about symbols and support them in working out the meaning and use of semiotic systems. The work of Coates and Coates (2006) has also shown how informal social and conversational exchanges between children and their peers during their multi-modal activities can offer practitioners' insights into how young children make sense of their worlds as they discuss matters of importance to them.

Valuing multi-modal representation

Hattingh (2011) has highlighted the importance of valuing children's' multi-modal activities. She notes the work of Freire, who contends that power relationships are particularly evident in education, where children may be reluctant to pursue their own interpretations of meaning if they are at odds with those expected by adults in the setting. Hattingh's research has shown that through multi-modal activities, children are able to make their own voices heard. Hattingh has also drawn on the work of Vasquez, who found that young children 'imagined that the social world could be otherwise' and that they could 'change the way things were' (cited by Hattingh, 2011). When children understand that their meaning-making endeavours are valued, this provides a driving force for their literacy development as they proactively devise different ways to represent their thinking.

Symbolic representation reflects young children's thoughts and feelings, hence its importance for early years practitioners. As Observers, we can be watchful of children as symbol-makers and symbol-users and be alert to signs of their symbolic behaviour. As Tolfree and Woodhead (cited in Clark, 2005: 36) note:

> It is not so much a matter of eliciting children's preformed ideas and opinions, it's much more a question of enabling them to explore the ways in which they perceive the world and communicate their ideas in a way that is meaningful to them.

By tracking young children's schemas and their multi-modal activities, we can record young children's gradual shifts from personal meaning-making to shared understandings of symbolic systems and use this to help create the kinds of experiences and resources that will enable children to represent their world in a variety of forms. Close observation of children's activities provides a window onto the way in which children think, act, and feel. Case Study 6.2 provides some examples of young children's mark-making and other multi-modal activities that reflect their developing symbolic representation.

Case study 6.2   Representations of meaning

Lone is an early years lecturer whose doctoral research focused on young children's capacity to demonstrate their identity and their meanings through their symbolic representations at home, in nursery, and at school. Her research has shown how using freely available resources, children's spontaneous and creative actions provide them with opportunities to draw on their own life experiences.

Role-play, drawings, cut-outs, selected artefacts, and found objects are some of the methods and contexts in which children are able to express their meanings. Their representations give an insight into the way they construct their world and make it visible: using what they know, calling on their own cultural experiences, and interpreting it in their own way. At times they combined their drawings, writing, and collage with role-play, toys, and other physical resources to represent their meanings symbolically.

In her research, Lone observed that children made choices from resources that surrounded them, and used these to represent their thinking in sometimes surprising and inventive ways. These resources included paper and pencils used in drawings, scribbles, and early attempts at writing; however, just as frequently, the modes of representation that the children used included the use of found objects and scraps of card, boxes or collage materials. Role-play was found to be an effective context for meaning-making, and was frequently combined with play that involved toys or rearranging objects or furniture, sometimes in combination with spontaneous mark-making. Children were found to engage in complex narratives in drawings and artefacts that may have appeared messy or trivial at first sight, but their meanings took on a complex and serious character when time was taken to listen to their accompanying descriptions or stories, or to observe their subsequent play and activities. This ability to express their thoughts and feelings is borne out in 4-year-old Joseph's drawing of his bear at nursery. What

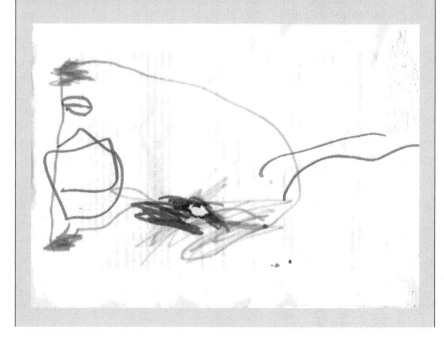

began as a drawing on scrap paper became a story about his bear who was fed through the hole in his stomach: the hole had appeared accidentally as he repeatedly drew his pen over the spot on the page. Joseph's resourcefulness in creating a narrative around this hole demonstrates his ability to problem-solve as he draws, and to represent his thinking in a 'principled' way as he interpreted and evaluated his drawing.

Children can find ways to make their own meanings visible if they are able to use their imaginations, and understand that their own means of representation are valued by those around them.

After a holiday in Spain, 7-year-old Ellen and her younger brothers re-enacted a bull-fighting scene at home using their toys, accompanied by a poster. They used this opportunity to reflect on cultural traditions related to bull fighting and to consider their own feelings about this.

It may appear problematic and uncomfortable to be receptive to the multiple interpretations and expressions of the children's representations which reflect the changing nature of the child's voice, creativity, and meanings in different contexts. However disorganized and chaotic children's representational activities might appear on the surface, Lone's research shows that there is a clear order and focus to the intentions and meanings within which the children were engaged as they worked and played.

(Hattingh, 2011)

The Observer in adult-initiated and child-initiated activities

Observing children can enable practitioners to be alert to their needs, interests, and achievements and, in doing so, they can use this information to guide their interactions 'in the moment' as well as to create further possibilities as they feed this information into the setting's OAP system or provision. The informal, spontaneous observations *in situ* help to ascertain whether formal, pre-planned observations are necessary, but the Observer will also be alert to opportunities for children and their caregivers to participate in observational activities to ensure that their perspectives are included and significant moments captured. Such significant moments include signs of emerging symbolic representational processes exhibited in children's symbolic behaviour and manifested in a range of multi-modal artefacts created by the children during both adult- and child-initiated activities. Taking a holistic perspective, one that encompasses personal, social, and emotional dimensions in the 'significant moments', we can tune into children's multi-modal expressions of meaning-making and find out about their friendships, how their identity is being constructed, what motivates and preoccupies them. Observation, then, is not only about noting the manifestations of children's internal representational or cognitive processes, it is also about understanding that learning is about social participation and occurs through mediated action and reciprocal relationships within specific cultural and historical contexts. Moreover, decisions made about 'significant moments' are essentially a process of interpretation and professional judgement that merges the Observer into the Assessor dimension of the adult role, as the following chapter illustrates.

Reflective questions and tasks
1. Examine the system of observation, assessment, and planning within a setting and consider how each aspect feeds the others within the cycle. How does the system benefit the child's progress?
2. How do you interpret the notions of child-centred and socially just observational practices?
3. Visit an early years setting and observe any evidence of young children's various modes of representing the world. What multi-modal representations are evident?
4. Consider how observational practices might empower or disempower children.

7 The Assessor

> There is a need to harness the dynamic power of educational assess-
> ment to motivate and empower learners.
>
> (Patricia Broadfoot)

This chapter focuses on the second phase of the OAP trilogy – assessment – and
the way in which observations are interpreted. Like observation, attention is
drawn to the need to clarify the purposes of assessment by recognizing how
differing perspectives on these purposes can generate different styles of assessment and the subsequent judgements that are made. It calls for the early years
practitioner to be cognisant of the power they hold in evaluating the evidence
they collect about children's needs, interests, and achievements and the judgements that are made whether these occur in the moment or for planning ahead.
We highlight how our assessment practices are driven by our own perspectives
on the assessment process, and how this in turn can be influenced by our
perceptions of children and how we construct our 'image of the child'. We
explore the importance of the socio-cultural context for assessment and the
impact this can have in formulating what we infer from our observations. We
consider how early years practitioners can help to generate socially just and
child-centred approaches to assessment practices that might empower young
children and assist them in developing an awareness of their own capabilities.

Some key features of assessment

One early years expert has defined assessment as 'the ways in which, in our
everyday practice, we observe children's learning, strive to understand it, and
then put our understanding to good use' (Drummond, 2003: 13). According to
official sources, assessments are essentially the judgements and decisions that
are made about children's learning and development on the basis of evidence

from observational material (QCDA, 2010). Whatever our perspective of assessment is, it will in many respects be framed by our statutory obligations.

Statutory requirements

The Early Years Foundation Stage (EYFS) states clearly that 'ongoing assessment is an integral part of the learning and development process' (DfES, 2007: 2.19). As we saw in Chapter 6, the evidence for this assessment comes from observations of 'day-to-day activities' in a range of contexts that are predominantly self-initiated by children, which are then used to plan for appropriate provision. This is considered to be 'formative assessment', otherwise known as assessment *for* learning. In England, at the end of the Foundation Stage, children are formally assessed against the early years goals across the six Areas of Learning and Development. This is known as the Foundation Stage Profile and is intended to offer both an end-of-stage summative assessment and act as a baseline assessment for Key Stage 1. Thus we are also compelled to undertake 'summative assessment', otherwise known as assessment *of* learning.

In addition, early years practitioners, together with other professionals working in children's services, are obliged to complete the Common Assessment Framework (CAF) to help identify any additional support that a child might need – Case Study 4.2 (pp. 62–3) provides an example of practitioners using the CAF forms. The early years practitioner has a preventative role to play here in terms of ensuring intervention before potential problems become serious.

As an Assessor we are therefore legally obligated to engage with both formative and summative assessment processes within our practice. These terms are invariably now referred to as 'assessment for learning' and 'assessment of learning' respectively. However, we suggest that distinguishing between the two is somewhat artificial, since there will always be an element of the 'summative' within formative assessments – a judgement is made at a particular moment in time, and in this sense it incorporates a summative element. Similarly, all summative assessments are invariably temporary and intended to be fed forward – the Foundation Stage Profile is a judgement of progress 'so far', and so provides a baseline for Key Stage 1 and assists in the transition process which continues throughout our education – it therefore incorporates a formative element.

Assessment as child-centred and socially just practices

We suggest that the Assessor can broaden his or her perception of assessment that meets statutory requirements but also undertaken in the spirit of fulfilling the twin agendas of *socially just* and *child-centred practices*. This means moving beyond perceiving assessment as a process of auditing to ensure progress or for the raising of learning standards. As Bertram and Pascal (2002: 92) put it, 'we live in an audited society where what is measurable is seen as significant. We need to ensure that what we are measuring truly matters and that we are not simply focusing on those things that are easily measured'. Like observations, the key to ensuring effective assessment is to ensure the purpose of the assessment is *valid, ethical and has value* not just for adults but for the children and their caregivers. We have a responsibility as an Assessor to ensure our assessments are clear, fair, and unprejudiced and are sensitive to the cultural and linguistic background of children (Dunphy, 2010). The Assessor will also recognize that assessment is a complex and, in many respects, an 'elusive process' and acknowledges 'the unpredictability of development' (Carr, 2001: 92). Indeed, Fleer (2002) maintains that as assessments are enacted in a social context, they are inevitably transient and fluid. Such views raise the question of whether children's achievements can ever be effectively 'measured'.

These issues are important ones for the Assessor to critically reflect upon, as they will help to generate a clearer understanding of the different perspectives of assessment that exist in practice. There has been much debate regarding the purposes and nature of assessment in the early years but if we are to incorporate the twin agendas of child-centred pedagogy and social justice within our practice, the Assessor needs to clarify how their statutory obligations can be accommodated within this framework of child-centred pedagogy and social justice. In the following section, we consider some of the different perspectives, which can help the Assessor to formulate their own understanding.

Perspectives of assessment

Accountability perspective

The idea of assessment as accountability proliferates in educational policy and practice driven by political motives to drive up standards. It focuses on viewing assessment as a tool for *measuring performance* that can be used to quantify quality and to delineate progress. In this perspective, assessment becomes a vehicle for defining the quality of a setting and places a premium on certain aspects of educational learning – invariably literacy achievement – and is a common trend across many countries, including the UK (Casbergue, 2010). The Foundation Stage Profile is an example of how assessment is used in the early years to provide benchmarks of performance, and has created much controversy regarding the expectations that are levelled on young children's abilities and the accompanying pressures these create for early years practitioners in striving to help children to meet such benchmarks or 'standards' (Rogers and Rose, 2007).

It is interesting to consider assessment practices elsewhere, which serve to illustrate the accountability perspective within early years provision in England and how the institutional context influences practice. For example, in Germany no such accountability assessment takes place. Beckerle (2009) has shown how early years practitioners 'are entrusted to be autonomously responsible for the final decision on the quality of children's education and care'. She goes on to say that 'although there are some organisational standards for early childhood education and care in Germany such as group sizes, there are almost no peda-gogical standards and existing curricula are not obligatory'. Her research has shown how these differences fundamentally affect the working routines of early years practitioners in the two countries, with practitioners in Germany having more flexibility and freedom.

The literature is prolific regarding the stresses and anxiety that account-ability assessment place on young children and its effects on their motivation, self-esteem, and evidence of disengagement with formal schooling (Alexander, 2010). Drawing on Vygotskian theory, Fleer (2002) has also drawn attention to how traditional assessments tend to focus on weaknesses rather than strengths and in this sense look backward rather than forward and project a *deficit model* of children's learning. As Drummond and colleagues put it:

> There is much more to assessment than diagnosing deficits or diffi-culties, labelling problems, and writing copious assessment profiles. Effective assessment means finding out what children have learned to know, do and feel, and then taking responsibility for a curriculum that builds on and enriches their learning.
>
> (Drummond et al., 1992: 4)

The flaws and consequences of accountability assessment have led to an alter-native model that adopts a *socio-cultural* perspective of assessment.

Socio-cultural perspective

Fleer has advocated a socio-cultural approach to assessment, moving away from traditional techniques that involve measuring individual acquisition of skills or knowledge to a focus on 'people's active changes of understanding and involvement in dynamic activities in which they participate' (Rogoff, cited in Fleer, 2002: 106). This perspective acknowledges the *interconnecting social and cultural worlds* of children. Similarly, Carr et al. (2005: 129–30) consider the purpose of assessment should be 'to notice, recognise and respond to compe-tent and confident learners and communicators'. Carr's (2001) perspective of assessment proposes that the purposes of assessment ought to be about enhancing learning rather than checking competency, about communicating with children, staff, and caregivers rather than monitoring and surveillance, and about envisaging children's potential rather than focusing on shortfalls. Carr writes that assessment needs to

> acknowledge the unpredictability of development, it will seek the perspective of the learner, a narrative approach will reflect the

learning better than performance indicators and collaborative inter-pretations of collected performances are helpful.

(Carr, 2001: 61)

As such it is a more 'authentic' form of assessment (Fleer, 2002).

A socio-cultural perspective of assessment therefore focuses attention on formative assessment or *assessment for learning*. Assessment is viewed in terms of reciprocal and responsive relationships and entails the sharing, negotiation, and revisiting of assessment practices in which children and their caregivers have some input. Socio-cultural views of assessment see it as a dynamic inter-action that focuses on processes and potential (Fleer, 2002). If, for example, we view learning as participation in a learning community rather than as the acquisition of skills and knowledge, this directs our attention to different issues and processes (Carr et al., 2005). Some of these issues and processes are discussed in the next section.

Understanding the contextual factors influencing assessments

Acknowledgement of social and cultural contextual factors that influence observations and assessments is strongly endorsed by the socio-cultural perspective of assessment with an emphasis on the individual in action with others rather than just a focus on the individual (Carr, 2001). One framework that offers a helpful way of ensuring assessment takes this into consideration is Bronfenbrenner's ecological systems theory. This theory rests on the belief that all children's social and cultural worlds are interconnected in a variety of ways.

Ecological systems theory

In Chapter 1, we introduced the *ecological systems theory* of human develop-ment and the various influences on a child's learning and development. You may recall that Bronfenbrenner (1979) envisaged a child's development in terms of the *interpersonal relationships* that the child encounters within a system of different and increasingly complex *environments* or layers of influence. These 'layers of influence' or 'environments' have been named the microsystem, the mesosystem, the macrosystem, the exosystem, and the chronosystem. According to Bronfenbrenner, it is the quality of the reciprocal relationships within these various systems that determines the quality of children's experi-ences and has a direct bearing on shaping human development.

The *microsystem* is the layer that is closest to the child and with which and with whom the child has direct contact such as the immediate family, the neighbourhood, and early years settings. It is the level within which a child experiences immediate interactions with other people, beginning with the home but expanding as the child matures to incorporate other relationships and environments. The early years professional becomes one of the reciprocal relationships within the growing microsystem encountered by the child. The *mesosystem* is less tangible, since it is conceived in terms of the connections between the various structures within the microsystem. The mesosystem comprises, for example, the interrelationships between child and parent and between parent and early years practitioner. The *exosystem* is easier to identify – this refers to the larger social system in which the child might not directly participate but still has the potential to impact on the child. For example, the parent's workplace is part of the exosystem which the child may never attend but which might affect the amount of time a child spends in childcare – the exosystem thus acts as an indirect force shaping what relationships the child encounters in the microsystem. The *macrosystem* is less visible, since it refers to cultural values, customs, and laws that exist within or directly and indirectly dictate how the microsystem and exosystem operate. The macrosystem might affect the child through cultural norms or ideological 'blueprints' that support a particular type of child-rearing practice or through legal frameworks such as the EYFS. The macrosystem also incorporates broader issues such as socio-economic status and ethnicity. The final 'layer' is the *chronosystem*, which is another less tangible but still influential system and relates to events and transitions related to time that occur within the child's life, such as maturational changes as the child grows older or more unexpected events such as the death of a parent. The chronosystem also entails wider socio-historical circumstances such as changes in equal opportunities for women and the impact of these on young children's circumstances today via increased working prospects and consequent childcare issues. In a recent review of the EYFS, Tickell (2010: 86) states that the EYFS reflects the Bronfenbrenner model, placing 'the unique child at the centre of the framework enabled by positive relationship and enabling environments which support the child's learning and development'.

Bronfenbrenner was strongly influenced by Vygotsky and his work also draws attention to the social relationships that young children encounter as well as the multitude of factors that might affect the nature and quality of these social relationships and the child's learning and development. Like Vygotsky (and Piaget for that matter), he envisaged children as active participants as they engaged with the world. Indeed, he emphasized *mutual* interaction as integral to human development and noted how disruptions in one system had a knock-on effect on others. He considered that such influences were 'bi-directional' – the relationships or structures within and between the different layers or environments are affected by and interact with each other.

Bronfenbrenner's model shows how we are located within historical, cultural, political, and social contexts and the early years practitioner needs to be aware not only of how they affect young children but how these different layers affect our own observations, assessments, and subsequent interactions with young children. So when evaluating any observation of a child, the Assessor will take into account the various factors that may have influenced or affected the child and consequently how the child engages with their world to a greater or lesser degree.

Furthermore, Fleer (2002) warns against only envisaging contextual factors as operating as social influences *on* the child. She draws on Rogoff's view that children's learning and development are not only constituted by the external socio-cultural context but they also *contribute to* and *participate in* that context. She states:

> The assessment paradigm is now ready to move from a view of focusing on individual thinking in a social context to thinking of assessment as not just located in the individuals – but rather as a dynamic organism which includes the education institution and its taken-for-granted practices, the cultural values and systems of knowledge which shape the children's world views, and the interactional processes, including mediation, between children, teachers and artefacts and systems.
>
> (Fleer, 2002: 117)

But within this framework of influencing factors, we must not forget the child. The next section highlights how the way we view children can fundamentally affect our interpretations.

Image of the child

Childhood as a social construction

Our image of the child is simply *how we view young children* – it refers to our attitudes towards them, how we think they should be treated, what we think they are capable of, and what we know about them. Such images dictate how a child is perceived not just by practitioners but by society as a whole. History has provided a spectrum of images of the child that can be found in the arts and literature – images such as 'the innocent child' or 'the sinful child'. The way in which children are portrayed in the arts and literature also denotes how susceptible images of the child are to subjective interpretations and has led sociologists to posit that the notion of childhood is *socially constructed* and that 'childhood is a social construction because of the specific ways in which very young children become socialised in different societies' (Gabriel, 2010: 138). Gabriel goes on to write that 'adults have developed powerful concepts of childhood which define the ways in which we think about children' (2010: 150). As Dahlberg et al. (1999: 43) put it: 'There is no such thing as "the child" or "childhood" . . . instead there are many children and many childhoods, each constructed by our own under-standings of childhood and what children are and should be'.

Early childhood as a foundation

Different conceptions of childhood offer early years practitioners the opportu-nity to reflect on their own image of the child and how other views 'fit' or ought to fit into their own perceptions. As in the past, there is a tendency to perceive children in terms of what they will become. We commonly use terms such as 'foundations' – particularly in the early years – to reflect a sense that childhood is a hidden part of something that only becomes visible later, like the founda-tions of a building. Such is view is known as the 'embryonic' model of the child – where children are considered to be in a state of transition into something more mature (Gabriel, 2010). This correlates with Piaget's 'developmental' child who passes through various stages of maturational development. Clearly, the maturational elements of young children's development are undeniable; however, the implication behind these perspectives of the child is that young children's immaturity renders them weak, dependent, vulnerable, incapable, and in need of protection. As Clark (2005: 45) puts it, 'viewing young children as weak, powerless and vulnerable may lead to high expectations of the adults's role in terms of protection and nurture but low expectations of children in terms of how they can express their perspectives, priorities and interests'.

Beings not becomings

Since the 1970s an alternative model of childhood has evolved from the field of sociology which views children as 'social actors' who form their own social group and should thus be viewed as 'beings' not 'becomings' (Quortrup, 1987). As James and Prout put it, children 'inhabit a world of meaning created by themselves and through their connections with adults' (cited in Gabriel, 2010: 138). James and Prout (1997) consider that children's ideas and choices are of interest in their own right and should not be conceived in terms of what they will become. Childhood is seen as a 'time in itself' rather than 'a time of prepa-ration' (Doddington and Hilton, 2007). Whitehead (2007: 277) offers a useful analogy to help clarify these ideas: 'Young children are not chrysalides waiting for the ultimate stage in their educational metamorphosis: they are human beings living their lives here and now.'

The constructivist child

It is easier to view children in the here and now when we take into considera-tion what we now know about young children's learning and development.

We have seen in previous chapters how children are now acknowledged as active agents in the construction of their own learning rather than passive recipients, and that the process of making sense of the world is one of active construction as individuals internalize their engagements with the physical and social environment and become 'makers of meaning' (Candy, 1991). Piaget was an early advocate of this constructivist approach to development, which gives a different image of the child to that of his 'developmental' model – here the dependent and vulnerable child becomes a proactive and competent individual capable of creating his or here own reality and culture.

The *constructivist child* correlates closely with the child-centred ideology that was introduced in our opening chapter. You will recall how the Plowden Report (Central Advisory Council for Education, 1967) heralded an image of the child as active, exploratory, curious, creative, playful, and sociable. Such a view is also endorsed by the socio-cultural perspective of the child as the previous section has noted and correlates with some of the images of the child presented by the EYFS (DfES, 2007), which refers to the child as 'unique', 'competent', 'resilient', 'capable', 'confident', and 'self-assured'.

Citizens now and citizens of the future

At the same time, tensions exist regarding other images that are presented by the EYFS of the child as 'vulnerable' and needing to be 'cared for' and 'feel safe'. So are we to prepare and protect children or are we to work co-constructively alongside them? Are young children dependents who need guidance or are they capable independent explorers? Perhaps an *interactive and inter-dependent* perspective is needed, as we saw in Chapter 3 in the discussion on the notion of a secure base and a safe haven – the two operate together providing both a basis from which to proactively explore and a retreat to return for comfort or reassurance – here the child is viewed both as an active agent and in need of protection. Nor need we necessarily decide for or against viewing children as a 'being' or 'becoming' but understand that they are both 'being' and 'becoming' – citizens now *and* citizens of the future (Alexander, 2010) – in the same way that as early years professionals we also exist as we are now, yet are on a pathway of becoming better practitioners.

We continue to be constructivists throughout our lifetime as we build upon and make sense of our experiences with the world into adulthood. This is the approach adopted by the Reggio Emilia educators who call for practitioners to not just 'consume' knowledge but to 'construct' it (Rinaldi, 2005a), and resonates with many of the points made in Chapter 2 and the idea of a learning community. If we accept that all learning and knowledge development is an ongoing process of constructive inquiry for both ourselves and for children and we take into account the socio-cultural view of learning as a process of interpersonal relations and view the child as an active agent, it is possible to conceive how we can be co-constructors and co-collaborators with young children making meaning and knowledge together (MacNaughton and William, 2004; Dunphy, 2010). But what are the implications of this for the Assessor?

We need to ensure our image of the child as a learner is 'in line' with our assessment practices (Carr et al., 2005). In Chapter 2, we highlighted the importance of early years professionals examining their own perceptions of their professional knowledge and this includes their image of the child. As an Assessor, we can clarify our own image of the child because how we envisage young children will directly influence the expectations we have of them and therefore how we judge them, as Case 7.1 demonstrates – this will help to identify the implicit and explicit power dimensions to assessment.

Case study 7.1   Image of the child

This case study provides an example of a mixed Reception/Year 1 teacher who fundamentally changed the way in which she judged children. It tells the story of 6-year-old Kieren who found it difficult to sit still on the carpet or to move about the classroom space without bumping into the furniture. Other children in the class called him 'clumsy' and although the teacher discouraged such 'name calling', she personally found him to be disruptive and boisterous most of the time. The teacher was finding it difficult not to feel negatively towards him and had to make a concerted effort not to let her negative feelings interfere with her professionalism and the way in which she interacted with him. She recognized that Kieren might have some attention problems and realized she needed to investigate his needs further, so she decided to observe him in different contexts, including the outdoor area where she discovered a completely different child. This became especially apparent during a class project on 'pirates'. Kieran seemed really interested in this and in one outdoor session he started to build a pirate ship out of large wooden blocks. He was quickly surrounded by other children who wanted to join in with the story. Kieran took the lead as 'director', showing other children where to place the blocks and assigning roles. Soon the ship was completed and a pirate ship adventure play began. The storytelling was rich and complex and included references to Peter Pan, Pirates of the Caribbean, and children's shared understanding of what pirates are. During the play Kieran became the master player, taking the lead, communicating his ideas effectively to other children, building relationships and staying focused for a sustained period; all things he found difficult to achieve in the indoor classroom.

From this observation and subsequent activities, the teacher was able to transform her image of Kieren and the assumptions she had about his capabilities. She recognized that her assessments of his learning prior to the outdoor observation were limited and framed around a particular perception that disguised his potential. She realized that her initial assessments had pre-judged her subsequent assessments regarding his learning in the classroom until she was able to see Kieren through a different 'lens'. This experience led her to re-evaluate her assessments and make more child-centred and fairer judgements. She was able to utilize her reassessments to create more opportunities for Kieren to express his capabilities and build on his interests and needs.

The power of assessment

The implicit and explicit dimensions of power

Rinaldi (2005b: 24) considers that assessment essentially involves 'deciding what to give value to'. Since assessment is about *making value judgements*, there is an implicit power dimension. At the very least, the act of judging another person implies some sense of superiority over that person. Moreover, traditional assessment practices invariably involve normalization, classification, and categorization and thus they have an adult-led, pre-set agenda that firmly puts the power of the assessment in the hands of the adult (Carr et al., 2005). The power this carries becomes legitimized through formalized assessment processes such as the Foundation Stage Profile, where norm-referenced criteria set up standardized expectations and measurements of what a child should aspire to, what is considered to be essential learning, and what is valued as being an achievement.

Even when assessment practices are more informal and child-centred, such as the system followed in Te Whāriki, where learning dispositions are the focus for assessment rather than performance indicators, *judgements are still made*. When observing a child's disposition, for example, an evaluation is made about whether the child is 'more or less disposed' towards the disposition and about whether children engage in dispositions 'more or less frequently, appropriately or skilfully' (Claxton and Carr, 2004: 88–9). If we consider the disposition named in the EYFS that refers to children being 'motivated to learn', a child can be considered to be intrinsically motivated but the *strength* of this motivation can change over time or with circumstances. Judgements are thus still made about the child's progress.

The inherent power of assessment is also expressed through the underlying values, beliefs, knowledge, and attitudes that direct the judgements being made – the *professional knowledge* that guides all decision-making. In addition to formal assessment criteria that structure the evaluation, all forms of assessment are based on an *implicit value system*, a set of beliefs about what children should do, say, feel, and be. In turn, our judgements are framed by our own cultural heritage and professional identities, as Chapter 2 showed, which will carry particular perspectives of assessment.

Another reason why assessment is about power lies in the potential consequences of assessment. The things we do and say when we assess young children's learning affect their feelings, their sense of self-worth, and their knowledge of themselves. The Te Whāriki curriculum, for example, acknowledges how assessments have a powerful influence on children's 'sense of themselves' (New Zealand Ministry of Education, 1996). Not only do assessments set up expectations, they can also lead to *labelling*. As Willan (2010: 68) puts it, 'the words we use can be powerful and emotive – they may even be damaging' – labels might be a useful way of summarizing a particular child's needs but they can disguise a more sophisticated understanding and neglect a complex range of issues. Armstrong (2003: 125) states that 'the label of "learning difficulties" is not a description to be applied to people but a category that disenfranchises people from participation in society as valued and equal citizens'.

Assessment dilemmas

Assessment is thus about power for many reasons. As Drummond et al. (1992: 9) note: 'The act of assessing is, in a sense, an expression of the power that we have over the children we work with, and their future lives.' Nonetheless, awareness of developmental expectations can help practitioners to be alert to the possibilities that some children may need additional support. We saw in the Introduction the significance of early intervention where assessment of possible issues is merited. Wolfendale (1997: 109) claims that there is 'a broad responsibility on the part of all early years practitioners towards the distinctive learning and developmental needs of all children, in creating opportunities for them to flourish'. In England, the EYFS tries to guard against practitioners pre-judging a child's capabilities by presenting children's developmental progress in six phases with a reasonable degree of overlap between them. This recognizes the differences that can occur between children of similar ages. Thomas (2008) posits a dilemma facing practitioners by noting that having large and overlapping age bands means that you might have unnecessarily high expectations for younger children but, on the other hand, having such a broad spectrum might lead a practitioner to become too relaxed about potential problems – this means we need to be both inactive and vigilant at the same time.

So how can we fulfil our responsibilities towards statutory obligations and children's potential needs while guarding against the implicit and explicit power consequences of assessment? Gipps (2002) argues for assessment opportunities and relationships that are based on power *with* rather than power over children, and the final section of this chapter considers some of the ways an empowering approach to assessment might be generated.

Empowering assessment

Collaborative assessment

One of the ways in which practitioners can diminish negative manifestations of the power of assessment is by developing collaborative approaches to assessment. Moss (2008: xv) has suggested that evaluation should be a collective process with 'the democratic formation of judgements of value'. In the previous chapter, we saw the Reggio Emilia approach to documenting children's work. What is significant about this approach is the way in which it is interpreted. This is a collaborative process between children, staff, and caregivers in which documented work is reviewed together and provides all involved with opportunities to revisit the work and reflect on the learning processes involved and the learning that has been developed. It can raise questions about the children's learning, alert staff to any issues, and provide a basis for further inquiry or discussion. MacNaughton and Williams (2004: 261) suggest that useful questions to pose during review and reflection of documentation include: What is similar and what is different in what we learn from different learners? What are the differences in how we each see what is significant? What learning seems worth exploring further? What actions do we want to take as a result of this review and reflection?

These questions are particularly helpful for ensuring assessment is *formative*. What makes it become formative in character is the way in which it feeds forward. This can occur via formal or informal assessments, *in situ* or via creative planning of adult-initiated activities on the processes or the products of learning. Research shows effective formative assessment directly impacts upon the quality of learning in early years settings particularly in the form of feedback given during interactive moments (Siraj-Blatchford et al., 2002). Such feedback has been called 'undocumented responding in responsive and reciprocal exchanges' (Carr, 2001: 174). We saw in Chapter 5 how part of being a Facilitator can involve the adult *commentating* on what the child is doing, on what is happening, and on aspects of the child's performance and attainment. This kind of feedback helps to 'specify and construct attainment and improvement' (Claxton and Carr, 2004: 93). But such discussion is an interactive exchange between Assessor and child and so feedback is also 'feedbetween' and becomes a mutual construction of attainment and improvement.

Since interpretation is ultimately a subjective process, the importance of communal interpretation helps us to guard against isolated and partial perceptions. Chapter 2 highlighted the importance of examining professional knowledge and part of this scrutiny involves opening it up to alternative 'lenses' that can occur through collaborative dialogue. Shared discussion with the children also helps to ensure their participation in the process and that their voices are heard – it becomes assessment *with* rather than assessment on children. As Rinaldi (2005b: 24) puts it, 'the result is knowledge that is bountiful and enriched by the contributions of many'. The children also come to see that not only do others value their work, but their contributions to valuing work are valued. It provides the 'authentic' assessment proposed by socio-cultural perspectives of assessment and is based on a pedagogy of 'listening and relationships' (Rinaldi, 2005b).

Self-assessment

Such collaboration engages children more directly in their own learning and stimulates self-assessment, enabling children to express and reconstruct their ideas, feelings, and understandings. Research on assessment procedures has shown self-assessment to be 'essential' to the assessment process (Black and William, 1998). Rinaldi (2005b) shows how documentation provides a basis to assess self-knowledge and it thus has implications for the development of metacognition, which was discussed Chapter 5. Thus, sharing documentation such as learning journeys with children means creating not only possibilities for more authentic assessment, but also provides a means for further learning. As Carr et al. (2005: 140) write, 'children who contribute to their own (and others') assessments are being perceived as competent and confident learners'. Self-assessment promotes a sense of ownership, responsibility, self-esteem, and gives practitioners the opportunity to gain a deeper insight into children's perspectives and thinking (Glazzard et al., 2010).

A view that perceives self-assessment as a 'rich site for learning' will embrace the flexible and open-ended nature of the assessment process rather than being restricted by pre-determined goals. These ideas link to the notion of *ipsative assessment* where the balance of power regarding assessment shifts entirely to the child. An ipsative approach to assessment will not rely on norm-referenced criteria for success, such as the Early Learning Goals of the EYFS, but will use the child's prior achievements for comparison with their present achievements to highlight their progress. The term 'ipsative' is derived from the Latin *ipse* ('of the self'), and therefore focuses on personal progress rather than expectations and criteria set by yourself rather than others. It has empowering potential similar to the way in which athletes set themselves the target of beating their own 'personal best'.

Personal learning journeys can be promoted along self-assessment and ipsative lines while group learning journeys can encourage collaborative assessment or peer assessment. Group review sessions of prior learning not only provide opportunities for children to self-assess, but to join in a communal discussion of peer assessment. Children can be invited to contribute their views and understanding of other children's efforts and experiences and generate meaningful discussion together. This is a similar process to the High/

Scope approach to early years provision that originated in America – children are actively encouraged to both plan and review their own activities and share ideas and experiences within a group context (OECD, 2004).

Positive assessment

Other ways we can ensure a more empowering approach to assessment is to frame our judgements in positive terms. Claxton and Carr (2004: 89–90) propose that judgements (or adverbs) about progress can be framed around the notions of 'robustness', 'breadth', and 'richness'. By 'robustness' they mean the strength of a child's progress can be judged in terms of how robustly a child continues 'to respond in a learning positive way' even when the activity become less conducive or supportive – for example, when building a tall tower that keeps falling down and the adult is not around to provide assistance. 'Breadth' refers to the increasing variety of domains in which 'positive learning responses' occur – this includes being able to transfer a skill used in one context to another such as fetching the scotch tape that had been used to make cardboard models to fix the tower blocks together. Finally, 'richness' entails the increasing sophistication of young children's responses and competencies as they develop more strategies, flexibility or more complex approaches towards the activities in which they engage. For example, a child can develop more creative ideas in trying to problem-solve how to make a tall tower that doesn't fall down, such as seeking help from a peer or using more blocks at the bottom to strengthen the foundations. Children can in effect become more 'ready, willing, and able' to persist in an activity, apply their developing skills and understanding across different contexts, and improve the complexity of their thinking.

Critical reflexive assessors

Finally, to help generate empowering assessment, the Assessor can ensure they incorporate a critically reflective approach to their practice. Warming (2005) has suggested that adults may never truly be able to represent children's experiences and 'voices'. Instead, drawing on others' work, she supports the notion of 'reflexive re-presentations', which acknowledges the way in which adults essentially re-present children's experiences and voices but they do so reflexively by taking into consideration children's 'different and contextualised voices' (Warming, 2005: 65). As Critical Reflectors and Assessors, we will be cognisant of our own and others' influences on our interpretation. We recognize that assessment is an analytical process, which requires us to pose questions regarding the observational material on which we are basing our judgements – questions such as 'what ideas are the children expressing?', 'what do their actions tell us about them?', 'what is significant about this evidence for the child?' It is about finding patterns, making associations, sifting out significant aspects, relating evidence to developmental knowledge and theory, interpreting behaviour, formulating conclusions based on informed judgements. Drummond suggests we should essentially ask ourselves, what can we see, how best can we understand what we see, and how can we put our understanding to good use? She goes on to remind us:

> The practice of effective assessment requires a thorough understanding and acceptance of the concepts of rights, responsibility and power, lying at the heart of our work as teachers. In searching for ways to make our assessment practices more effective, we are committing ourselves to recognising children's rights, shouldering our responsibilities towards them, and striving to use our power wisely and well.
>
> (Drummond, 2003: 178)

Case study 7.2   The OAP cycle and empowering assessment

Emma is Head of Nursery at Puddleduck Hall Day Nursery in Gloucester. She provides an example of how learning journeys are incorporated into the OAP cycle at her setting and how they are used to provide a vehicle for effective, meaningful, and empowering assessment for learning. She writes:

In our nursery for 2–5-year-olds we use a combination of group and individual learning journeys to document children's interests and learning, using these as the basis of our OAP system. The group learning journeys regularly feed into a child's individual learning journey facilitating our personalized planning. We have found that combining different interests makes it more manageable to support a greater range of observed interests. One such example was a key person noting that two of her children who had been engaged in some of the pirate imaginative play were also interested in the concept of floating and sinking. These interests were combined and we talked bout how pirate ships floated. This led onto children exploring a range of materials to investigate if they floated or sank. Some of the children used available resources to make their own pirate ship, exploring the properties of materials such as which ones floated, were waterproof, etc.

In terms of our assessment practice, essential ingredients include our key person approach, partnership with parents/carers and the sensitive enabling relationships and interactions we have with our children. Staff observe children all the time, regularly partaking in children's play and learning but it is children's significant moments that are used to support assessments of children's learning and development. These 'moments' are documented by key persons in children's group and/or individual learning journeys, called 'look at all our learning', and inform the direction that learning experiences will take. Our learning journeys are working documents and are part of children's regular review on their own interests and development and though this reflective process, next steps are created collaboratively between children and staff. Parents/carers are also encouraged to share children's learning journeys regularly, also providing their own 'magic moments' of their child's interests and learning.

One example to illustrate the above was an observation of a significant moment made by a key person of Ella, aged 3 years, 2 months. Ella preferred to play alone and moved away when peers approached. The key person had observed Ella showing interest in watching a group of children who were using cardboard boxes as boats with spades as oars. The key person sensed Ella's desire to join in but also her reluctance and went and sat in a box near where Ella was watching. The positive relationship the key person had with Ella gave Ella the confidence to move closer and eventually climb into the box, still watching the other children. The key person asked Ella what they needed and Ella said 'spade', pointing to the other children using spades. Ella was not willing to get a spade herself, so the practitioner moved away to find one but on observing Ella, she noticed that another girl, Beth, approached with two spades. She gave one to Ella and then joined Ella in the box with her own spade. The significant moment came when Ella did not move away from Beth and the box, but smiled and started to paddle her 'oar'. The two girls shared this experience, sometimes saying, 'faster!' or 'pirates coming!' for a further ten minutes. The key person watched from a short distance and took a photograph of Ella sharing her box boat with Beth.

Later that session, Ella helped develop the photograph and put it in her learning journey. The key person asked Ella who she was sharing her boat with and Ella replied 'Beth', pointing to Beth across the room. The key person then asked if Ella would like to show Beth and at that moment, Ella picked up her learning journey and took it over to Beth to show her. We felt that this was a significant moment in Ella's social development and this assessment was later documented alongside the photograph and shared with Ella's dad when he came to collect her. Ella's key person talked to Ella and her dad, explaining that Ella had shared her boat, starting the reflection and then sensitively encouraging Ella to explain the rest of the experience, thus engaging Ella in reflection of her own learning.

The Assessor in adult-initiated and child-initiated activities

Like observations, assessment should be embedded in practice and 'woven into the fabric of classroom activity and interaction' (Carr, 2001: 157). The Assessor will be cognisant of the many dimensions to the assessment process including how their interpretation is shaped by the interconnected web of influences on the child, their own image of the child, and the various responsibilities they have for evaluating children's progress. In doing so, they can seek opportunities for generating more empowering ways of assessing children, which will encourage children's participation in initiating their own activities. Assessors recognize the particular value of formative assessment *in situ*, since this will shape our interactions and what we initiate in the moment. At the same time, such assessments will help to define the opportunities we can create for extending young children's development, as the next chapter illustrates.

Reflective questions and tasks

1. Outline your own image of the child – what values, attitudes, beliefs about young children does this image project?
2. What assessment practices have you experienced and how have these affected your own experiences of learning?
3. How necessary is it to be judged by a set of external standards?
4. What assessment practices can you adopt that will enable and empower children?

8   The Creator

What children learn does not follow as an automatic result from what is taught . . . Rather, it is in large part due to the children's own doing as a consequence of their activities and our resources.

(Loris Malaguzzi)

This chapter brings us to the last part of the OAP cycle envisaged as the Creator self. We have chosen this term deliberately in place of the term 'planner' to emphasize the creative dimension of the adult role in early years settings and the need to create a contextually and developmentally appropriate learning environment for all young children, taking into account the cultural, linguistic, and developmental diversity that exists in every early years setting. We give particular emphasis to creating a playful learning environment and discuss three key aspects of play – heuristic play, pretend play, and outdoor play – that can help to ensure a playful enabling environment. In doing so, we highlight the importance of creating multi-sensory, active, embedded, imaginative, and explorative experiences that cater for children's diverse needs and interests and address the twin aims of socially just and child-centred practices.

Planning as a co-constructed process

We begin from the premise that planning for young children's learning in early years settings is a highly creative practice. This concept we believe applies to all early years settings, from childminders who provide for children in their own homes to large group settings including schools that cater for the early years phase. All adults working in early years settings, whatever the size or nature of the group, will be engaged in creative acts of observation-led planning for appropriate provision. Drake (2009: 7) describes early years provision as a structure 'which scaffolds children's learning but also allows them the freedom to experiment, investigate and pursue personal interests'.

Co-construction of an enabling environment

However, we would want to go further than this to suggest that rather than a scaffolding structure, which is fixed and rigid, the enabling environment is *co-constructive* – that is, it is flexible, permeable, and responsive. Co-construction was discussed in relation to the Facilitator self, to promote inter-subjectivity in the pedagogic relationship (see Chapter 5). We suggest also that the concept of co-construction can be applied to the process of creating and planning the environment and that if children are engaged in shaping the nature of provision, their experiences will be more meaningful. We would apply this principle to all children from birth onwards. As we have argued throughout this book, participation is not age dependent. Even newborn babies can participate in the decision-making process of the setting if we are tuned into the ways in which they communicate their needs and interests to us. Working with young children in this way is challenging, however. But through the critically reflective practice and the professional confidence this can bring, we believe reciprocal and co-constructive approaches, in which adults share control of the environment and intentions for learning with the children, provide the starting point for creating an enabling learning environment.

A child-initiated and adult-initiated enabling environment

We know from many decades of robust research that young children learn best in an environment that encourages them to engage in extended episodes of child-initiated play. After all, play is described widely in the literature as a *voluntary* activity, free from externally imposed rules and adult expectations. Therefore, the idea of planning for play or making provision for adult-initiated play might seem a contradiction in terms. Nonetheless, while it might not be possible or desirable to plan for specific learning outcomes in play, it is possible to create an environment that enables children to experience high-quality play activities that may have been initiated by children or by adults that still reflect the life-enhancing, social, imaginative, and affective qualities that play can generate.

Underpinning good practice is the fundamental principle that any curriculum, irrespective of the age group, should be broad, balanced, and relevant. To this we would add a child-centred and socially just curriculum provision. Within early years settings, planning is likely to operate at different levels and these different levels are considered below.

The statutory curriculum

Many countries have established statutory or recommended curricular frameworks. How these are interpreted will inevitably be influenced by adults' knowledge, values, beliefs, and principles for young children's learning, which in turn influence how and what children learn. According to the Early Years Foundation Stage (EYFS) (DfES, 2007):

- Providers must plan and organize their systems to ensure that every child receives an enjoyable and challenging learning and development experience that is tailored to meet their individual needs.
- Providers must have effective systems to ensure that the individual needs of all children are met.
- Providers must ensure that there is a balance of adult-led and freely chosen or child-initiated activities through indoor and outdoor play.
- Providers must undertake sensitive observational assessments in order to plan to meet children's individual needs.

The intended, offered, and received curricula

Moving beyond statutory curricular guidelines, the *intended curriculum* is described in policies, long- and medium-term plans. Most group settings will have local policies and plans to ensure a cohesive and consistent framework for children's progression. However, while they may guide adults in the process of planning, in practice there will be significant variations in interpretation and enactment. This is the *offered curriculum*, understood as what adults actually *do* in the setting, how they set up provision, activities and how they interact with children. Directly related to the offered curriculum is what we might call the *received curriculum*, which is what children actually learn and how they respond to the planned provision and activities.

As many research studies have shown, the difference between the offered and received curriculum can be stark (Adams et al., 2004; Rogers and Evans, 2008), where there is a mismatch between adults' and children's intentions. This is particularly true in play activities that might be heavily prescribed by adults with little room for children's agency in determining the direction and content of the play. Flexibility and responsiveness are therefore necessary and are key characteristics of the Creator dimension to the adult role. The provision of suggestive props and ideas – commonly referred to as *provocations* – which provoke children's interest and curiosity are more effective in stimulating play than pre-specified themes or topics.

The hidden curriculum

Finally, there is the *hidden curriculum*, which is understood as the *implicit messages* given by the environment, along with the values, attitudes, and behaviours of all those who are part of the setting. Messages, both positive and negative, can be conveyed in the images and texts that adorn the walls and notice boards of corridors and rooms as well as in the resources that are used. The extent to which parents and caregivers are welcomed into the setting and how information is communicated will ultimately influence the children's learning experience, sense of belonging, and well-being. The hidden curriculum is of particular relevance if we are to ensure socially just provision.

Achieving a balance between adult-initiated and child-initiated activities

Child-initiated activity is understood as activity led by the child inspired by his or her interest in a particular idea or object. In contrast, adult-initiated activity is understood as activity that is planned by the adult with a specific learning intention in mind. However, there will still be some flexibility as the adult and child interact in a *co-constructed* way. It is here that we might see examples of scaffolding or sustained shared thinking discussed in Chapter 5. In adult-initiated activities, adults exercise judgement about how best and to what extent they should or need to lead or guide children, when to step back and when to support. In practice, we would suggest that the boundaries between child- and adult-initiated activity are *blurred* and frequently *overlap* in the course of an activity or session. In child-initiated play, for example, an adult might be invited to participate or might see an opportunity to join in the play. The key point in this instance is to follow children's lead rather than impose ideas on the developing play episode. Similarly in adult-initiated activities, children may suggest new directions and inject new ideas into the interaction that the adult can then follow. Adults in early years settings may unthinkingly sanction or censor children's ideas about the world, encouraging what seems to be educationally sound, and discouraging children from acting creatively. Adults may make decisions about what is educationally relevant and useful as they plan play activities *for* children. An obvious example of this is the way in which adults may select the themes and resources for children's role-play and are surprised to find that children are not interested in the beautifully presented and elaborately resourced activity, as Case Study 8.1 illustrates.

Case study 8.1   Children creating a playful environment

This story recounts the experiences of one of the author's observations of children's play in a Reception class.

A Pet Shop had been set up for a period of three weeks. The teacher had prepared the children well with stories and visits. She preferred not to take a direct role in the children's play but directed groups of children to play in the 'Pet Shop'. Typically, the children entered the role-play area, breaking into pairs or

---

individuals in unrelated activity, moving objects and chatting. Play that could be related to the Pet Shop was brief and perfunctory.

On one particular occasion, Holly emerged as the leader of the play (which after only a few minutes was visibly disintegrating). There followed a period of tremendous activity while Holly began to construct a kitchen in the Pet Shop – I should perhaps tell the reader at this point that the teacher had moved the kitchen/home equipment out of the role-play area (now the Pet Shop), and although it remained adjacent to the area it had been packed away and was 'out of bounds'.

Holly moved the table, laid it, and set about preparing an imaginary meal. The other children quickly joined her and began to adopt family roles. This bout of domestic play lasted for over 15 minutes. The level of social interaction and language use was more sustained and more complex than in any of the Pet Shop play I had observed. I was curious to know what Holly thought about this play. I asked her to tell me about it. Why had she given up on the Pet Shop idea? She said, 'because the Pet Shop is closed today, and so we are at home having tea'.

This was, of course, an entirely plausible answer. Yet I was struck by her body language, which suggested to me that my question had engendered a feeling of guilt, that I had somehow caught her out and discovered her subversion. Without wanting to overstate or misinterpret this brief example of role-play, I am persuaded that the children were not remotely interested in the Pet Shop theme, that it may even have precluded creative role-play activity taking place had Holly not seized the initiative.

(Rogers, 2007)

The issue of balance between adult- and child-initiated activity is a common concern. The EYFS recommends a balance of 50:50. But we would encourage practitioners to use their knowledge about the children to guide their judgement in deciding what the balance should be, recognizing that this will shift over time and according to the particular context.

Creating an enabling environment

As mentioned previously, debates about what constitutes an appropriate curriculum and pedagogy for young children frequently refer to the tensions that exist between the place of subject knowledge and the role of play in early learning, the balance between adult- and child-initiated activities, and the extent to which adults can and should plan for learning outcomes. These debates feature across the globe in a range of diverse countries and educational systems and although there are clearly local and cultural differences, there are some key principles and features that appear to characterize early years provision internationally. These were described in previous chapters in relation to the Facilitator, Carer, and Communicator selves. To reiterate, young children need to be active, physically and intellectually; play occupies a central place in young children's repertoire of learning approaches and children need significant others to help them make sense of the world, to feel valued and cared for. 'Enabling Environments' is one of the four interconnected themes of the EYFS (DfES, 2007). Within enabling environments there are four commitments that highlight the importance of observing children in the planning cycle and emphasize the need for adults to 'create a stimulating environment that offers a range of activities which will encourage children's interest and curiosity, both indoors and outdoors' (DfES, 2007).

Extending the theme of a flexible, permeable, and responsive approach to planning, Claxton and Carr (2004) identify four types of environment that adults can create for young children:

- a prohibiting environment
- an affording environment
- an inviting environment
- a potentiating environment.

Different interpretations of an enabling environment

According to Claxton and Carr (2004), a *prohibiting* environment is tightly controlled by adults and provides an activity schedule where there is little time for children to be engaged over any length of time. In this kind of environment, adults may inadvertently discourage children's positive dispositions. An example of this is where a 'carousel' of activities is laid out by adults and the children are allowed a fixed period of time at each activity before moving on to the next. An *affording* environment is one that offers children an array of opportunities but with few deliberate strategies on the part of adults to draw children's attention to potential learning opportunities. An example of this is a nursery where there is much freedom for children to play with a wide range of materials, but little adult involvement, co-construction or episodes of sustained shared thinking. An *inviting* environment is one that not only affords the opportunity for learning but is one in which adults draw attention to its value and interest. An example of this is a kindergarten where adults and children co-construct the activities and where adults engage in meaningful conversations with children about what they are thinking and feeling. Finally, *potentiating* environments identify children's dispositions but also actively 'stretch' and develop them. Potentiating environments, Claxton and Carr (2004: 92) argue, involve frequent participation in shared activity and 'share the power between teachers and learners'.

Drawing on the work of Wenger (1998), Claxton and Carr (2004) suggest that adults need to balance two main processes in creating and sustaining a potentiating learning environment. The first of these is 'reification', which means to make experiences concrete in some way. An example in an early years context would be to document and make visible others children's learning, perhaps through annotated drawings and photographs. The second process is 'participation', which resonates with the central focus of this book that places relationships at the heart of the learning process and the development of shared understanding between adults and children and between children. To some extent, the model proposed by Claxton and Carr (2004) points towards more recent conceptualizations of relational pedagogy (Papatheodorou and Moyles, 2009) and the pedagogy of listening (Rinaldi, 2005a) mentioned at various points throughout this book, and links also with a concern for early years education and care to be child-centred and socially just at its core. In a similar vein, Goleman (1995) identifies seven 'ingredients' that are critical to children developing confidence as learners, and that will enable them to capitalize on opportunities to develop skills, knowledge, and competence across a range of subject domains and activities:

- confidence
- curiosity
- intentionality
- self-control
- relatedness
- capacity to communicate
- cooperativeness.

Positive learning dispositions

Similarly, Lilian Katz's work on positive dispositions, now widely disseminated, offers a way for early years practitioners to think about creating opportunities for children to become life-long learners. Katz (1993) defines a disposition as a tendency to exhibit frequently, consciously, and voluntarily a pattern of behaviour that is directed towards a broad goal. According to Katz, the developmental question is not just 'what can children do?' Rather, it is also 'what should children do that best serves their development and learning in the long term?' Establishing positive dispositions is significant in learning for life because it allows consideration of other attributes that affect learning, such as motivation. The acquisition of facts, knowledge, and skills is not in itself enough to secure learning. For example, most children have the capacity to listen, but they may or may not have the disposition to be listeners (Katz, 1993). Dispositions are not learned by children through formal instruction but are nurtured by people, contexts, and the environment that surrounds them

– dispositions are 'caught rather than taught' (Dowling, 2006: 92). Katz aptly describes dispositions as 'habits of mind, not mindless habits' (Katz, 1993).

A key question for adults, particularly in creating and planning for children's learning, is 'what dispositions should adults encourage, strengthen?' And related to this, a second question is suggested: 'What dispositions should adults model in their practice?' This second question is challenging. Early years practitioners work in an increasingly regulated context, where pressure to prepare children for formal schooling, meet externally imposed targets, and satisfy parental expectations – which may not align with the setting's principles – can lead to a loss of professional confidence and the implementation of practices that may inadvertently undermine the development of positive dispositions; for example, an over-emphasis on the acquisition and performance of literacy skills through inappropriately long and passive phonics sessions. While it is possible to argue that the children may be learning something about letters and sounds, they are unlikely to be learning a disposition to read or to become life-long learners (Bertram and Pascal, 2002). Summarizing why it is important to nurture dispositions in early childhood curriculum programmes, Dowling (2006) notes that:

- Newly acquired knowledge and skills will only be secured in learning if they are used.
- The way in which something is taught may either strengthen positive attitudes or damage them.
- Dispositions are not easy to regenerate once they are extinguished.
- Positive dispositions for learning should be strengthened as opposed to dispositions for performance.

All this reminds us that planning for or creating provision does not automatically mean that learning will take place or that children will become confident learners. This depends on the nature of the adult's interactions with children and the nature of the provision offered. What also appears to be central for such provision is the place of play.

The place of play

Play lies at the heart of the early years curriculum, endorsed by the EYFS. Creating play opportunities that engage children and foster positive dispositions requires that adults are tuned into children's interests and inclinations, and that they possess a deep understanding of the contribution of play to children's learning and well-being. How you view play, its value and its benefits to young children will inevitably shape the experiences you offer, the extent to which the play is structured through resources and themes, and how much you are a part of the play. Practice will vary between settings and types of settings. For example, research (Brooker et al., 2010) has highlighted the very real differences between the play experiences of children in nursery settings on the one hand and reception class settings on the other, although children may be of the same age or very close in age and subject to the same curricular framework, such as the EYFS. The nature of the play offered and experienced by children will also depend on the nature of resources available, on access to space, and availability of funds. Whatever age or type of setting, children need extended periods of time for play *without interruption* to encourage complex forms of play, persistence, engagement, planning, and the exercise of social skills such as negotiation and cooperation. Agreeing and establishing rules and roles in play takes time. Constant interruptions will discourage children from engaging in complex play episodes. When play is used as a 'holding task', while the adults attend to other activities and children are called from play to read or change book bags, this signals to children that play is of less value than other activities.

Understanding and sharing the significance of play

The value of play in human development and experience is beyond dispute, but *how* precisely play contributes to human development is still open to debate (Smith, 2010). Extensive research across many disciplines and decades has shown that play has value in the developing child in the sense that it appears to be mainly enjoyable and meaningful, and that it is frequently social. Indeed, from birth babies search for meaning though social and increasingly playful interactions with caregivers and family members (Carpendale and Lewis, 2006). Play is a universal human activity, observed across diverse cultures (Goncu et al., 2006).

However, how play is viewed and valued by adults will vary and depend also on the way in which children and childhood are positioned within a culture or society. Global migration and the culturally diverse populations of children that characterize many early years settings in the UK and elsewhere mean that early years practitioners cannot assume that play will be appreciated by all parents or for that matter all children. Brooker (2010) writes of the need to develop shared understandings of play and learning between practitioners and parents. Similarly, Gupta (2010) writes of the deeply held appreciation of children's play in Indian society, yet its place in early childhood education and school is less valued by adults. Recognizing different cultural perspectives on play in the early years setting is critical to ensure that all children benefit from the opportunities that play affords.

Much has been written about play in early development and there are many excellent texts that provide detailed accounts of the role of play in early learning and development. The focus in this chapter is on the importance of creating an environment that enables children to play in ways that are appropriate to their level of competence so that they gain a sense of fulfilment and achievement and are able to realize their ideas within a supportive, co-constructive pedagogy.

Developmental play

Play takes on many forms and functions across the early years and indeed the lifespan. Knowing how play changes as children grow, learn, and develop is important in creating an enabling environment. The dominant types of play observed in young children are usually described as sensori-motor play (babies to toddlers), constructive play (from 12 to 18 months), symbolic play (from 2 to 3 years), and socio-dramatic play (from 3 to 4 years) (Smilansky and Shefatya, 1990). These categories are useful because they enable adults to provide appropriate materials and contexts to encourage and support the types of play children are most likely to engage in at particular points in their development.

However, by following these developmental stages too rigidly we may miss some of the other kinds of play we see in children from birth onwards. For example, you will have seen babies and young infants putting objects in the mouth, which is highly sensitive at this time (MacIntyre, 2001), grasping and sucking and exploring the properties of new objects with intense concentration. It would be easy to conclude that the preferred type of play was solitary and exploratory. However, babies also engage in and initiate highly social interactions and games, enjoying repetition, rhythms, and actions with key persons and caregivers alike. In a similar vein, we know that for children aged 3–5 years, pretend play is the dominant form of play. However, children in this age group also engage in intensive bouts of exploratory play and constructive play, often showing their interests through schemas as described in Chapter 6. In providing appropriately for children we need to keep an open mind and think of development stages and milestones as flexible and overlapping, remembering too that context is also instrumental in determining how and in what ways children respond to playful materials and encounters with others.

Heuristic play

Young babies engage in bouts of sensory and exploratory play and construct schemas that relate to cause and effect, objects and space through movement and crucially through interaction with others (Athey, 1990). As babies are able to sit up and manipulate objects, the world takes on a different perspective and they gain greater independence in their play. This is when the Creator might introduce 'treasure baskets' – collections of a range of objects in a basket that provide multi-sensory experiences and encourage opportunities for hand/eye coordination. Treasure baskets open up opportunities for the baby to engage with objects that they might otherwise not be able to explore. The idea of treasure baskets, first suggested by Elinor Goldschmeid (1987), is extended into the play of toddlers through the provision of 'toddler bags', which contain different types of resources for the toddler to investigate. The emphasis in the heuristic play of toddlers and babies is on sensori-motor play through exploration. Although Goldschmeid affords the adult a passive rather than active role in heuristic play, she argues that the presence of the adult is significant because it enables the child to engage fully in exploration within a safe context with the adult acting as a secure base and safe haven for the child. The work of Dowling (2006) suggests a more interactive role for the adult during heuristic play that can offer many opportunities for sustained shared thinking through both verbal and non-verbal communications with babies and toddlers of the kind suggested in the Chapters 4 and 5.

Pretend play

Another aspect of play that is of particular importance in creating an enabling environment is an appreciation of the significance of *pretence and role-play* for young children. Research from a range of theoretical perspectives concludes that pretend play or role-play is the preferred activity of social engagement in children aged 3–5 years (Corsaro, 1997; Harris, 2000; Dunn, 2004; Carpendale and Lewis, 2006), and that it provides a meaningful context within which young children can develop and exercise social skills and competence (Sutton-Smith, 1971). Pretend play in the under-3s is often linked with the achievement of object permanence in the first year and with the development of a *theory of mind* (Astington, 1993). This is an essential human life skill, marking an important milestone in children's development (Dunn, 2004) and underpinning the beginning of empathy, aptly described by Baron-Cohen (2003: 26) as a 'leap of imagination into someone else's head', as Chapter 3 has shown. Social interaction and social referencing are vital in this process, as we saw in Chapter 4. Infants in the first year of life do not engage in pretend play in ways that are recognizable to us (Gopnik et al., 1999; Harris, 2000). Then, in the second year of life, we see the emergence of pretence, which, as it develops over the next few years, becomes increasingly complex and varied in content and style.

The roots of more complex role-play can be traced to the early mental representations formed by young infants, a process that begins from birth and is manifested as children demonstrate increasing understanding of object permanence, from 6 to 9 months. Put simply, infants begin to 'hold' images of objects and people in their heads, even in their absence. Clearly, this capacity is present very early in the first few months of life. But to *use* those representations deliberately as in pretence is not evident until well into the second year, when children are observed engaging in simple imitative play with the emergence of symbolic activity, such as using a banana as a telephone. To do this, the child needs to have some understanding of two worlds – the world in which the banana is just a banana, and the world in which the banana can also become a telephone (Rogers and Evans, 2008), or in Vygotsky's (1978) words 'the stick becomes a horse'.

Vygotsky's theory of play occupies a central position in his general theory of development (Newman and Holzman, 1993), although it is contained in one brief chapter (Vygotsky, 1978). His theory proposes that 'play is not the predominant feature of childhood but it is a leading factor in development' (Vygotsky, 1978: 101). In Chapter 5, Vygotsky's concept of the zone of proximal development (ZPD) was introduced. The point was made that the way in which Vygotsky conceptualized the ZPD in relation to children's play was very different to how he conceived of it in the teaching and learning relationship. First, Vygotsky proposed that the 'imaginary situation' is characteristic of all play and not simply of what we call role-play or fantasy-play activity. A second and related feature of play, and one that is closely linked with the creation of an imaginary situation, is the presence of rules: 'whenever there is an imaginary situation in play, there are rules – not rules that are formulated in advance and change during the course of the game but ones that stem from an imaginary situation' (Vygotsky, 1978: 95).

Vygotsky gives the example of a child playing the role of mother. The child, he suggests, is bound by the rules of what it means to be a mother, not only in the sense of a particular mother (for example the child's mother), but rather within the rules of 'maternal behaviour' (Vygotsky, 1978: 95). So children generalize their knowledge of mothers to a typical mother who needs to behave in a particular way for children to communicate to each other within the play frame. At the same time, Vygotsky argues, when children engage in games with rules (and here he gives the example of chess), they are still enacted within an imaginary situation. He concludes that 'just as we are able to show . . . that every imaginary situation contains rules in a concealed form, [so] the reverse – that every game with rules contains an imaginary situation in a concealed form' (Vygotsky, 1978: 95–6). Children's play changes over time as they gather more experiences, develop theory of mind skills and greater physical dexterity.

For Vygotsky, there is an important transition from young children's play, in which rules are secondary to imagination, to the games of older children, in which the imagination is subservient to rules (Vygotsky, 1978: 96). However, a significant developmental shift takes place as the child begins to engage in symbolic activity. The child at play is bound by the rules of the game (whether playing 'mother' or a game with rules); he or she is positioned between his or her desire to act spontaneously on the one hand and by the inherent need to subordinate those desires to the rules of the game on the other. If children do not 'play the game' within the boundaries of the imaginative frame and rules of the roles and game, the play will not be sustained. This is why Vygotsky

(1978: 99) contends that 'the child's greatest control occurs in play'. This is of profound importance in our understanding of role-play's contribution to children's development. There is no mention of curriculum subjects or academic achievement as such. Rather, the real benefit of play is that it enables young children to demonstrate, practise, and simply experience self-control and self-regulated behaviour. The rule-bound nature of play and the self-control children require in play so that the play is sustained, emphasize the importance of play between children who are more or less knowledgeable. In this way, his explanation of play differs markedly from the instructional relationship he proposes in relation to the ZPD.

Research and theory suggest that pretend play can help children develop self-control and insights into the perspectives of others. It enables children to confirm or challenge their own perspective on phenomena: 'the ability to imagine themselves taking a position that is different from their own' (Carpendale and Lewis, 2006: 39). Thus creating opportunities for such play between children promotes social learning, and recognizing how play changes over time is a key aspect of creating an enabling environment. To illustrate, James aged 2 takes his new toy car and 'drives' it over the sofa imitating the sound of a car saying 'broom, broom'. Liam aged 4½ builds a car out of large blocks. He calls to his friends, 'C'mon let's get in and go'. Prince and Sherry get in the car and head off on a journey to 'catch a baddie'. The difference in the type of car play observed demonstrates how play changes as children develop the ability to engage in more complex social play.

We have highlighted two distinctive ways in which children play at different points in the early years phase and for which early years settings need to provide time and space – heuristic and pretend play. Case Study 8.2 offers an example of how settings can provide these kinds of playful opportunities, even in very simple forms.

Case study 8.2   Creating opportunities for open-ended play

Sarah and Vanessa both own their own private nursery (Play Away and Hugo and Holly Day Nurseries) and were interested in exploring ways of creating opportunities for open-ended play, as they believed it provides a medium for powerful learning to take place. This was because they had noticed that the effectiveness of playful provision was at times haphazard in their settings. For example, children would discover their play had been 'tidied' away or that activities had been arranged and set out for them to play with by a well-meaning member of staff who had determined what the outcome should be – the resources looked beautiful but were remote from the children's thinking and activity in which they had previously been engaged. It was clear that they did not fully appreciate the importance and relevance of the children's play or their role within it. They were compartmentalizing the children's play and imposing an adult-led agenda on it, giving the message to the children that their play was less important than the adult's organization of it. Taking this concern forward, Sarah and Vanessa decided to focus on how to enable their staff to have a greater understanding of play.

They carried out the same activity in the two nurseries, which involved placing large pieces of material in each of the playrooms and observing what happened when the children were given the opportunity to initiate their own play. They recorded excerpts of the play and used them as a focus for a staff meeting to initiate discussion. The children demonstrated that they could play autonomously in a way that they had not been able to do in some of the more adult-led activities. They used this as a starting point to discuss the notion of empowerment as key to supporting children's development. The older preschool children sustained play for half an hour and used their imaginations to turn the material into a wide range of items such as building dens and for dressing up. The interactions were rich between children as they laughed together, worked together, learning from each other's experiences; they showed increased confidence and a wide range of social skills. The staff talked about the complexity of skills needed for imaginative play in a group situation. The provocation was also the basis of interesting discussions about the development of the imagination and whether there are ages and stages to this development. The toddlers loved the material and ran around with it. They enjoyed the way they could move with the material in an unstructured way. The babies loved feeling the material with their hands and feet and playing peek-a-boo with it. They enjoyed looking through it and tried to touch the face on the other side. They benefited from the open-ended nature of the material as a resource. The heuristic resources and open-ended opportunities that have subsequently been created in the playrooms have enabled the children to explore, discover, make links, and freely investigate. This work has inspired the staff and helped them begin to develop an understanding of open-ended play as a powerful learning experience and for questioning and challenging, rather than just accepting the way the nursery is run and established.

Outdoor play

It is now widely accepted that young children need regular, daily opportunities to play and learn outdoors. This presents some challenges to early years practitioners, since they are required to plan for and manage two distinctive yet related environments. For some adults, the challenge may extend even further to their personal attitude towards the outdoors. Children need adults who enjoy the outdoors and value the benefits it brings. However, inclement weather and the often physical, risky, and boisterous nature of outdoor play can be off-putting for some adults. Risk-taking is not only characteristic of outdoor play but of play more generally, as children explore ideas and materials, and try out new experiences (Tovey, 2010). But for many adults, the physical dimension of outdoor play can create genuine anxiety and concern. We know that children need to take risks in a carefully managed environment but that adults' anxiety about the dangers of being in the outdoors with very young children can lead them to over-emphasize the risk thus limiting children's opportunities to engage in challenging play.

In describing discourses of risk, Tovey (2010) notes that notions of risk may also be gendered, where physical play is more acceptable for boys than girls, and also embedded in cultural values about what is considered appropriate or inappropriate for young children. And yet risk-taking is a vital part of life. Tovey found that practitioners showed an aversion to risk and a reluctance to allow risk-taking in play. Feelings of anxiety and concerns about children's safety were common. Similarly, a study of outdoor learning in Foundation Stage and Year 1 classes by Waite et al. (2011) found that the dominant form of interaction in the outdoor areas was for the purpose of preventing risk. In creating and planning for an enabling environment, adults need to work with risk and recognize its importance and value in children's learning and skills development. Tovey (2010) suggests that rather than risk assessment, we need to embrace risk as an essential part of play pedagogy.

In keeping with the overriding message in this chapter, children need time, space, and flexible resources to develop outdoor play that allows for risk-taking, but it should not become the main focus of planning for the outdoor play. The outdoors offers a range of different learning opportunities and characteristics to the indoors, not least because it offers children freedom to be more active, noisy, and exploratory than is possible in indoor spaces (see Case Study 7.1, pp. 112–13). Such activity offers young children a range of multi-sensory, first-hand experiences such as feeling the effects of the weather and related temperature, the textures and smells of natural materials such as ice, earth, water, and wood.

Caring play

One final point: throughout this book we have emphasized the need for adults to create strong and secure relationships with the children in their care. This is particularly important if they are to develop secure and lasting attachments to significant others (Elfer, 2006). For example, secure relationships are vital to the development of play in babies and playful interactions between the key person and baby are a more powerful spur to learning than elaborate toys (Gopnik et al., 1999). All playful opportunities that are created are therefore framed around the idea of *caring* relationships, as discussed in Chapter 3.

The Creator in adult-initiated and child-initiated activities

As a Creator, the early years practitioner can create provision that gives children real choices about where, with whom, what, and how they play. He or she can create spaces both indoors and outdoors that allow for uninterrupted time to play, to revisit, rebuild, and recreate ideas. The adult can engage with all the dimensions of their adult role to show children that he or she is interested in their play and is an advocate for their play. We have suggested also that adults can consult and negotiate with children as co-constructors of the curriculum and pedagogy, which stimulates and supports their play. Through observation, verbal and non-verbal feedback, adults act as knowledgeable observers, assessors, carers, communicators, and facilitators, which may provoke them to initiate activities with the children or simply help to create provision that empowers all children to self-initiate in an enabling environment.

Reflective questions and tasks

1. What is your understanding of the notion of 'creating an enabling environment'?
2. What are some of the hidden messages in a play-based curriculum that might inhibit socially just practices?
3. Consider how play changes as children get older – how do they demonstrate progression in the complexity of their play and their increasing capacity to imagine, to represent, and to cooperate in their play?
4. Visit an early years setting and observe how the setting creates playful learning opportunities.

9 Conclusion

In this book, we have proposed seven key dimensions or 'selves' which characterize the adult role in early years settings and which relate in particular to the adult–child interactional relationship. This combination of selves we have called the *plural practitioner* to illustrate the many different but inextricably related aspects of the adult role. We do not want to present these as a fixed and final version; there may be other aspects that we have not covered and that readers would like to add. However, in our deliberations with each other and the students who provided a spur for the writing of this book, we agreed to settle on the seven selves that we believe embrace much of what is significant in the complex and intricate work that takes place in early years settings. We have made it clear throughout that in early years settings we are, often simultaneously, acting as Critical Reflector, Carer, Communicator, Facilitator, Observer, Assessor, and Creator of enabling spaces and places for children to learn and develop.

Each chapter has explored the particular nature of the interactions and relationships that are developed between adult and child and has in different ways emphasized particular features of each of the seven 'selves' that might help to enhance the quality of these daily interactions and the relationships that are built up around them. In doing so, we have acknowledged that young children learn 'from, through and with other people' (Claxton, 1999: 227). We have also proffered a view that the plural practitioner is guided by two important agendas: child-centred and socially just practices. By 'child-centred' we are not referring to the kinds of *laissez-faire* practices that assign little role to the adult other than to provide an appropriately stimulating environment while the child acts as the 'lone scientist'. Rather, we have suggested instead that we need to develop a robust pedagogy that places children's interests – both individual and collective – at its heart. In this way, we are 'child-centred'. We believe this to be a worthy aim for the twenty-first century where children continue to live in poverty even in affluent and technologically advanced societies. Early years education can and does make a profound difference to the lives of young children across the globe. Strong and secure relationships with caring adults who support and challenge children's emergent thinking is the key driver in the early years setting.

Similarly, socially just practices are fundamental not just to our own society but globally as well. As Alexander (2010: 4) puts it, 'we may need to act locally but we must be prepared to think nationally and indeed globally'. Early childhood education is increasingly a global concern and is accompanied by increased investment and interest by Western governments, as well as international organizations such as UNESCO and the World Bank (Pearson and Degotardi, 2009). Davis (2009: 239) has pointed out that 'early childhood is a high leverage area with investments in young children having the potential to reap big rewards into the future'. Indeed, investment in early education 'will help children develop the social, emotional, and academic foundations that will serve them throughout life' and provide long term benefits for 'a better prepared workforce, increased employment opportunities, stronger growth, and rising standards of living, while society will benefit from less crime, enhanced schools, and children who are better prepared to participate in democratic processes' (Committee for Economic Development, 2006: 1).

To support these agendas, the book has drawn on many perspectives including developmental psychology, neuroscience, and socio-cultural perspectives. Each perspective has something to offer and we take the view that an integrated approach to theory offers a strong basis for understanding how children learn and how adults can support them. Neuroscience, for example, has given added impetus to developmental psychology by showing how early experiences and interactions fundamentally affect the architectural development of the brain, placing significant importance on the adult's role in providing the most effective and stimulating learning environments. Research from this perspective has deemed the staff within early years settings to be the most important determinants of the impact that early childhood education and care will have on young children (NSCDC, 2007). Socio-cultural perspectives have shown how the contexts of children's learning influence and shape educational experiences and outcomes. Thus, throughout this book we have argued for a contextually and culturally sensitive approach to early years practice, one that draws on a range of theoretical perspectives.

In taking up the concept of the 'plural practitioner', we have tried to highlight the complexity of the adult role when working with young children and their families. We have deliberately left discussion of leadership and management to others (see, for example, Aubrey, 2007), since our focus is on the interactional relationship between adults and children and the potential of this to promote socially just and sustainable futures. Co-constructive, participative, and relational pedagogies can help to facilitate the powerful potential presented by young children in contributing to a sustainable society and ensure the generation of *professional capital*. Roberts and Roberts (2007: 4) suggest that

'sustainable development is concerned with the maintenance and enhancement of five types of capital', namely natural, human, social, manufactured,
and financial capital. The notion of professional capital has its roots in both
human and social capital, since it is concerned with the capacity building of
individuals to meet the needs of society in the context of professionalised
networks. It is both 'productive' and 'purposive' (Brodie, 2003) through its
intention to improve early years provision and to contribute to communities
of practice in children's services.

A recent report that considered the contribution early childhood education can make to a sustainable society emphasizes raising the training and
status of early years professionals as a 'high priority policy concern' (Pramling
Samuelsson and Kaga, 2008), not least because young children are particularly
vulnerable to adversities such as poverty and family breakdown and the care
given to them will be of particular importance. The UK government has
recently acknowledged the importance of professional capital in laying the
foundations for lifelong learning and life-chances. Public spending on the
early years in the UK has been markedly increased and is now above the OECD
average (OECD, 2009) with a significant proportion being channelled into the
establishment of a graduate-based profession in early childhood education.
Previously, very few regulations existed in the UK to guide early years provision and few or no professional qualifications were required. The radical altera-
tions in the structure and delivery of early years education and care have been
directed by the Every Child Matters initiative (DfES, 2004) and the establishment of a statutory curricular framework for 0–5-year-olds, the Early Years
Foundation Stage (DfES, 2007), to which we have referred throughout this
book. The move towards a graduate workforce with the introduction of the
Early Years Professional Status in 2006 by the Children's Workforce
Development Council, was based on the premise that higher level knowledge
and skills can lead to better outcomes for children and was driven by substan-
tive international research that revealed the benefits of effective early intervention (Schweinhart et al., 1993; Sylva et al., 2010). These developments recognize
the role of the plural practitioner in helping to create an inclusive, democratic,
and enlightened society and it is this commitment that lies at the heart of this
book and, we would argue, the heart of early years practice.

References

Adams, S., Alexander, E., Drummond, M.J. and Moyles, J. (2004) *Inside the Foundation Stage*. London: ATL.

Ainsworth, M., Blehar, M., Waters, E. and Wall, S. (1978) *Patterns of Attachment*. Hillsdale, NJ: Erlbaum.

Alexander, R.J. (2010) *Children, Their World, Their Education*. London: Routledge.

Allen, G. (2011) *Early Intervention: The Next Steps*. London: Cabinet Office.

Anderson, G.L., Herr, K. and Nihlen, A.S. (1994) *Studying Your Own School*. Thousand Oaks, CA: Corwin.

Armstrong, D. (2003) *Experiences of Special Education*. London: RoutledgeFalmer.

Arnold, C. and the Pen Green Team (2010) *Understanding Schemas and Emotion in Early Childhood*. London: Sage.

Astington, J.W. (1993) *The Child's Discovery of the Mind*. Cambridge, MA: Harvard University Press.

Athey, C. (1990) *Extending Thought in Young Children: A Parent–Teacher Partnership*. London: Paul Chapman.

Athey, C. (2007) *Extending Thought in Young Children*. London: Paul Chapman.

Aubrey, C. (2007) *Leading and Managing in the Early Years*. London: Sage.

Bandura, A. (1977) *Social Learning Theory*. Englewood Cliffs, NJ: Prentice-Hall.

Barer-Stein, T. (1987) Learning as a process of experiencing the unfamiliar, *Studies in the Education of Adults*, 19(2): 87–108.

Baron-Cohen, S. (2003) *The Essential Difference*. London: Penguin.

Barratt-Pugh, C. and Rohl, M. (eds) (2000) *Literacy Learning in the Early Years*. Buckingham: Open University Press.

Bartley, M. (ed.) (2006) *Capability and Resilience: Beating the Odds*. London: Department of Epidemiology and Public Health, University College London.

Bath, C. (2009) *Learning to Belong: Exploring Young Children's Participation at the Start of School*. London: RoutledgeFalmer.

Beckerle, C. (2009) Comparing the working routines of early years practitioners in Germany and England – a case study. Unpublished masters thesis, Frankfurt University.

Bennett, N., Wood, E. and Rogers, S. (1997) *Teaching through Play*. Buckingham: Open University Press.

Berk, L.E. (2003) *Child Development*. Boston, MA: Pearson Education.

Bertram, C. and Pascal, A.D. (2002) Assessing young children's learning: what counts?, in J. Fisher (ed.) *Building Foundations for Learning*. London: Paul Chapman.

Bertram, T. and Owens, S. (2007) Raise your game, *Nursery World*, 107(4074): 10–11.

Black, P. and William, D. (1998) Assessment and classroom learning, *Assessment in Education*, 5(1): 7–74.

Blakemore, S.-J. and Frith, U. (2005) *The Learning Brain: Lessons for Education.* Oxford: Blackwell Publishing.

Blenkin, G. and Kelly, V. (eds.) (1988) *Early Childhood Education: A Developmental Curriculum.* London: Paul Chapman.

Bourdieu, P. (1977) *Outline of a Theory of Practice.* Cambridge: Cambridge University Press.

Bowery, E. (2008) Is there a place for the discrete teaching of thinking sills and dispositions in a pre-school curriculum? Unpublished dissertation, University of Gloucestershire.

Bowlby, J. (1969) *Attachment and Loss, Vol. 1: Attachment.* New York: Basic Books.

Bowlby, J. (1988) *A Secure Base: Clinical Applications of Attachment Theory.* London: Routledge.

Bradbury, H. (2007) Social learning for sustainable development: embracing technical and cultural change as originally inspired by The Natural Step, in A.E.J. Wals (ed.) *Social Learning Towards a Sustainable World.* Wageningen: Wageningen Academic Publishers.

Brainethics (2006) *Bowlby's Bulb* [online]. Available at: http://brainethics. wordpress.com/2006/09/23/bowlbys-bulb/ [accessed 19 May 2011].

Brodie, P. (2003) *The invisibility of midwifery: will developing professional capital make a difference?* Sydney: University of Technology Sydney [online]. Available at: http://utsescholarship.lib.uts.edu.au/space/handle/2100/339?show=full [accessed 2 April 2010].

Bronfenbrenner, U. (1979) *The Ecology of Human Development: Experiments by Nature and Design.* Cambridge, MA: Harvard University Press.

Bronfenbrenner, U. (2005) *Making Human Beings Human: Bioecological Perspectives on human Development.* Thousand Oaks, CA: Sage.

Brooker, L. (2010) Constructing the triangle of care: power and professionalism in practitioner/parent relationships, *British Journal of Educational Studies*, 58(2): 181–96.

Brooker, L., Rogers, S., Ellis, D., Hallet, E. and Roberts-Holmes, G. (2010) *Practitioner Experiences of the EYFS.* DFE-RB029. London: DfE.

Brookfield, S. (1987) *Developing Critical Thinkers.* Milton Keynes: Open University Press.

Brookfield, S. (1995) *Becoming a Critically Reflective Teacher.* San Francisco, CA: Jossey-Bass.

Bruce, T. (2010) (ed.) *Early Childhood: A Guide for Students*, 2nd edn. London: Sage.

Bruner, J. (1986) *Actual Minds, Possible Worlds.* Cambridge, MA: Harvard University Press.

Bruner, J. (1990) *Acts of Meaning.* Cambridge, MA: Harvard University Press.

Candy, P.C. (1991) *Self-direction for Lifelong Learning.* San Francisco, CA: Jossey-Bass.

Caplan, H., Cogill, S., Alexandra, H., Robson, K., Katz, R. and Kumar, R. (1989) Maternal depression and the emotional development of the child, *British Journal of Psychiatry*, 154: 818–22.

Carpendale, J. and Lewis, C. (2006) *How Children Develop Social Understanding*. Oxford: Wiley-Blackwell.

Carr, M. (2001) *Assessment in Early Childhood Settings*. London: Paul Chapman.

Carr, M., Jones, C. and Lee, W. (2005) Beyond listening: can assessment practice play a part?, in A. Clark, A.T. Kjorholt and P. Moss (eds) *Beyond Listening: Children's Perspectives on Early Childhood Services*. Bristol: Policy Press.

Carr, W. and Kemmis, S. (1986) *Becoming Critical: Education, Knowledge and Action Research*. London: Falmer Press.

Carruthers, E. and Worthington, M. (2006) *Children's Mathematics: Making Marks, Making Meaning*. London: Sage.

Casbergue, R.M. (2010) Assessment and instruction in early childhood education: early literacy as a microcosm of shifting perspectives, *Journal of Education*, 190(1/2): 13–20.

Central Advisory Council for Education (England) (1967) *Children and Their Primary Schools* (The Plowden Report). London: HMSO.

Children's Workforce Development Council (CWDC) (2007) *Guidance to the Standards for the Award of Early Years Professional Status*. Leeds: CWDC.

Children's Workforce Development Council (CWDC) (2010) *The Common Core of Skills and Knowledge: At the Heart of What You Do*. Leeds: CWDC.

Christensen, P. and James, A. (eds) (2000) *Research with Children*. London: Falmer Press.

Clark, A. (2005) Ways of seeing: using the Mosaic approach to listen to young children's perspectives, in A. Clark, A.T. Kjorholt and P. Moss (eds) *Beyond Listening: Children's Perspectives on Early Childhood Services*. Bristol: Policy Press.

Clark, A. and Moss, P. (2001) *Listening to Young Children: The Mosaic Approach*. London: NCB/JRF.

Clark, A. and Moss, P. (2005) *Spaces to Play: More Listening to Young Children Using the Mosaic Approach*. London: NCB.

Claxton, G. (1999) *Wise Up: Learning to Live the Learning Life*. London: Bloomsbury.

Claxton, G. and Carr, M. (2004) A framework for teaching learning: the dynamics of disposition, *Early Years*, 24(1): 87–97.

Coates, E. and Coates, A. (2006) Young children talking and drawing, *International Journal of Early Years Education*, 14(3): 221–41.

Cohen, D. (2006) *The Development of Play*. London: Routledge.

Committee for Economic Development (2006) *The Economic Promise of Investing in High-Quality Preschool: Using Early Education to Improve Economic Growth and the Fiscal Sustainability of States and the Nation*. A Statement by the Research and Policy Committee of the Committee for Economic Development. Washington, DC: CED.

Cooper, R.P. and Aslin, R.N. (1994) Developmental differences in infant attention to the spectral properties of infant-directed speech, *Child Development*, 65: 1663–77.

Corsaro, W. (1997) *The Sociology of Childhood*. Thousand Oaks, CA: Pine Forge Press.

Cortazzi, M. (1993) *Narrative Analysis*. London: Falmer Press.

Craft, A. and Paige-Smith, A. (2008) What does it mean to reflect on our practice?, in A. Paige-Smith and A. Craft (eds) *Developing Reflective Practice in the Early Years*. Maidenhead: Open University Press.

Dadds, M. (1995) *Passionate Enquiry and School Development*. London: Falmer Press.

Dahlberg, G. and Moss, P. (2005) *Ethics and Politics in Early Childhood Education*. London: RoutledgeFalmer.

Dahlberg, G., Moss, P. and Pence, A. (1999) *Beyond Quality in Early Childhood Education and Care*. London: Falmer Press.

Daniels, D. and Shumow, L. (2003) Child development and classroom teaching: a review of the literature and implications for educating teachers, *Applied Developmental Psychology*, 23: 495–526.

Davis, J. (2009) Revealing the research 'hole' of early childhood education for sustainability: a preliminary survey of the literature, *Environmental Education Research*, 15(2): 227–41.

Department for Children Schools and Families (DCSF) (2008a) *Every Child a Talker*. Nottingham: DCSF.

Department for Children Schools and Families (DCSF) (2008b) *Independent Review of Mathematics Teaching in Early Years Settings and Primary School* (The Williams Review). Nottingham: DCSF.

Department for Education and Skills (DfES) (2004) *Every Child Matters*. Nottingham: DfES.

Department for Education and Skills (DfES) (2007) *Statutory Framework for the Early Years Foundation Stage*. Nottingham: DfES.

Dewey, J. (1998) *Experience and Education: The 60th Anniversary Edition*. West Lafayette, IN: Kappa Delta Pi.

De Wolff, M.S. and van Ijzendoorn, M.H. (1997) Sensitivity and attachment: a meta-analysis on parent antecedents of infant attachment, *Child Development*, 68: 571–91.

Doddington, M. and Hilton, M. (2007) *Child-centred Education: Reviving the Creative Tradition*. London: Sage.

Donaldson, M. (1978) *Children's Minds*. London: Fontana.

Dowling, M. (2005) *Young Children's Personal, Social and Emotional Development*. London: Paul Chapman.

Dowling, M. (2006) *Supporting Young Children's Sustained Shared Thinking: An Exploration* (Training Materials). London: Early Education (The British Association for Early Childhood Education).

Drake, J. (2009) *Planning Children's Play and Learning in the Foundation Stage*. London: David Fulton.

Drummond, M.J. (1998) Observing children, in S. Smidt (ed.) *The Early Years: A Reader*. London: Routledge.

Drummond, M.J. (2003) *Assessing Children's Learning*. London: David Fulton.

Drummond, M., Pouse, D. and Pugh, G. (1992) *Making Assessment Work*. London: NCB.

Dunn, J. (2004) *Children's Friendships: The Beginnings of Intimacy*. Oxford: Wiley-Blackwell.

Dunn, J., Brown, J., Slomkowski, C.T. and Youngblade, L. (1991) Young children's understanding of other people's feelings and beliefs: individual differences and their antecedents, *Child Development*, 62: 1352–66.

Dunphy, E. (2010) Assessing early learning through formative assessment: key issues and considerations, *Irish Educational Studies*, 29(1): 41–56.

Dweck, C.S. and Leggett, E. (1988) A social-cognitive approach to motivation and personality, *Psychological Review*, 95(2): 256–73.

Edgington, M. (2005) *The Foundation Stage Teacher in Action*. London: Sage.

Edwards, A. (2000) Looking at action research through the lenses of sociocultural psychology and activity theory, *Educational Action Research*, 8(1): 195–204.

Edwards, A. (2001) Researching pedagogy: a sociocultural agenda, *Pedagogy, Culture and Society*, 9(2): 161–86.

Eisner, E.W. (1998) *The Enlightened Eye: Qualitative Enquiry and the Enhancement of Practice*. Englewood Cliffs, NJ: Prentice-Hall.

Elfer, P. (2006) Exploring children's expressions of attachment in nursery, *European Early Childhood Education Journal*, 14(2): 81–96.

Elliott, J. (1993) Professional education and the idea of a practical educational science, in J. Elliott (ed.) *Reconstructing Teacher Education*. London: Falmer Press.

Evangelou, M., Brooks, G., Smith, S. and Jennings, D. (2005) *Birth to School Study: A Longitudinal Evaluation of the Peers Early Education Partnership*. London: DfES.

Feldman, R., Greenbaum, C. and Yirmiya, N. (1999) Mother–infant affect synchrony as an antecedent of the emergence of self-control, *Developmental Psychology*, 35: 223–31.

Field, F. (2010) *The Foundation Years: Preventing Poor Children Becoming Poor Adults*. London: Cabinet Office.

Fisher, R. (1998) Thinking about thinking: developing metacognition in children, *Early Child Development and Care*, 141: 1–15.

Fleer, M. (2002) Sociocultural assessment in early years education – myth or reality?, *International Journal of Early Years Education*, 10(2): 105–20.

Fleer, M. (2005) Developmental fossils – unearthing the artefacts of early childhood education: the reification of child development. *Australian Journal of Early Childhood*, 30(2): 2–7.

Fleer, M. (2006) The cultural construction of child development: creating institutional and cultural intersubjectivity, *International Journal of Early Years Education*, 14(2): 127–40.

Fonagy, P., Gergely, G., Jurist, E. and Target, M. (2004) *Affect Regulation, Mentalization and the Development of the Self*. London: Karmac.

Freeman, R.G. and Vakil, S. (2007) The pedagogical experiences and practices of family child care providers, *Early Childhood Education Journal*, 35(3): 269–76.

Fullan, M. (1993) *Change Forces: Probing the Depths of Educational Reform*. London: Falmer Press.

Gabriel, N. (2010) Adults' concepts of childhood, in R. Parker-Rees, C. Lesson, J. Willan and J. Savage (eds) *Early Childhood Studies*. Exeter: Learning Matters.

Gadamer, H.-G. (1989) *Truth and Method*. London: Sheed & Ward.

Geake, J.G. (2009) *The Brain at School: Educational Neuroscience in the Classroom*. Maidenhead: Open University Press.

Gilligan, C.F. (1982) *In a Different Voice*. Cambridge, MA: Harvard University Press.

Gipps, C. (2002) Sociocultural perspectives on assessment, in G. Wells and G. Claxton (eds) *Learning for Life in the Twenty-first Century*. Oxford: Blackwell.

Glazzard, J., Chadwick, D., Webster, A. and Percival, J. (2010) *Assessing for Learning in the Early Years Foundation Stage*. London: Sage.

Goldschmeid, E. (1987) *Infants at Work* (VHS video). London: National Children's Bureau.

Goldstein, L.S. (2002) *Reclaiming Caring in Teaching and Teacher Education*. New York: Peter Lang.

Goleman, D. (1995) *Emotional Intelligence*. New York: Bantam Books.

Göncü, A., Jain, J. and Taermar, U. (2006) Children's play as cultural interpretation, in A. Göncü and S. Gaskins (eds) *Play and Development: Evolutionary, Sociocultural and Functional Perspectives*. Mahwah, NJ: Lawrence Erlbaum Associates.

Gopnik, A., Meltzoff, A. and Kuhl, P. (1999) *How Babies Think*. London: Weidenfeld & Nicolson.

Gore, J. (1987) Reflecting on reflective teaching, *Journal of Teacher Education*, 38(2): 33–9.

Goswami, U. and Bryant, P.E. (2007) *Children's Cognitive Development and Learning. Research Survey for the Cambridge Primary Review*. Cambridge: University of Cambridge.

Gottman, J. and DeClaire, J. (1997) *How to Raise an Emotionally Intelligent Child*. New York: Fireside.

Gottman, J.M., Katz, L.F. and Hooven, C. (1996) Parental meta-emotion philosophy and the emotional life of families: theoretical models and preliminary data, *Journal of Family Psychology*, 10(3): 243–68.

Gupta, A. (2010) Play and pedagogy framed within India's historical, socio-cultural and pedagogical context, in S. Rogers (ed.) *Rethinking Play and Pedagogy in Early Childhood: Concepts, Contexts and Cultures*. London: Routledge.

Harris, P. (2000) *The Work of Imagination*. Oxford: Blackwell.

Hart, R. (1992) *Children's Participation: From Tokenism to Citizenship*. Florence: UNICEF International Child Development Centre.

Hattingh, L. (2011) Representations of meaning. Paper presented at UKLA International Conference, University of Chester, July.

Hirsch, D. (2007) *Chicken and Egg: Child Poverty and Educational Inequalities*. London: Child Poverty Action Group.

Hoffman, L.W. (2000) Maternal employment: effects of social context, in R.D. Taylor and M.C. Wang (eds) *Resilience Across Contexts*. Mahwah, NJ: Erlbaum.

Hooven, C., Gottman, J.M. and Katz, L.F. (1995) Parental meta-emotion structure predicts family and child outcomes, *Cognition and Emotion*, 9: 229–64.

Hutchin, V. (2003) *Observing and Assessing for the Foundation Stage Profile*. London: Hodder & Stoughton.

Hyland, N.E. (2010) Social justice in early childhood classrooms: what the research tells us, *Young Children*, 65(1): 82–7.

James, A. and Prout, A. (1997) *Constructing and Reconstructing Childhood*. London: Falmer Press.

Jones, E. and Schoon, I. (2008) Child behavior and cognitive development, in K. Hansen and H. Joshi (eds) *Millennium Cohort Study*. London: Centre for Longitudinal Studies.

Jordan, B. (2009) Scaffolding learning and co-constructing understandings, in A. Anning, J. Cullen and M. Fleer (eds) *Early Childhood Education: Society and Culture*. London: Sage.

Katz, L. (1993) *Dispositions as educational goals* [online]. ERIC Digest. Available at: http://ericae.net/edo/ED363454.htm [accessed 2 October 2011].

Katz, L. and Chard, S. (1989) *Engaging Children's Minds: The Project Approach*. Norwood, NJ: Ablex Publishing.

Katz, L. and Chard, S. (1996) *The Contribution of Documentation to the Quality of Early Childhood Education*. ERIC Digest, April EDO-PS-96-2.

Katz, L.F., Gottman, J.M. and Hooven, C. (1996) Meta-emotion philosophy and family functioning, *Journal of Family Psychology*, 10(3): 284–91.

Kelly, V. and Rose, J. (1996) Action research and the early years of education, *Early Years*, 17(1): 41–6.

Kincheloe, J.L. (1991) *Teachers as Researchers: Qualitative Enquiry as a Path to Empowerment*. London: Falmer Press.

Klein, L. and Knitzer, J. (2006) *Effective Preschool Curricular and Teaching Strategies*. Pathways to Early School Success, Issue Brief No. 2. New York: National Centre for Children in Poverty, Columbia University.

Klinnert, M., Campos, J., Sorce, J., Emde, R. and Svejda, M. (1983) Emotions as behavior regulators in infancy: social referencing in infancy, in R. Plutchik and H. Kellerman (eds) *Emotion: Theory, Research and Experience, Vol. 2. Emotion in Early Development* (pp. 57–85). New York: Academic Press.

Knott, G. (1979) Nonverbal communication during early childhood, *Theory into Practice*, 18(4): 226–33.

Knowles, G. (2009) *Ensuring Every Child Matters*. London: Sage.

Kress, G. (2000) *Before Writing: Rethinking the Paths to Literacy*. London: Routledge.

Kugelmass, J.W. and Ross-Bernstein, J. (2000) Explicit and implicit dimensions of adult–child interactions in a quality childcare center, *Early Childhood Education Journal*, 28(1): 19–27.

Kumpfer, K.L., Whiteside, H.O., Ahearn Greene, J. and Allen, K.C. (2010) Effectiveness outcomes of 4 age versions of the strengthening families program in state-wide field sites, *Theory, Research and Practice*, 14(3): 211–29.

Laevers, F. (1994) *Defining and Assessing Quality in Early Childhood Education*, Studia Pedagogica Leuven: Leuven University Press.

Lave, J. and Wenger, E. (1991) *Situated Learning: Legitimate Peripheral Participation*. Cambridge: Cambridge University Press.

Liston, D.P. and Zeichner, K.M. (1990) Reflective teaching and action research in preservice teacher education, *Journal of Education for Teaching*, 16(3): 235–54.

MacIntyre, C. (2001) *Enhancing Learning through Play*. London: David Fulton.

MacNaughton, G. and Williams, G. (2004) *Teaching Young Children: Choices in Theory and Practice*. Maidenhead: Open University Press.

Markus, J., Mundy, P., Morales, M., Delgado, C.E.F. and Yale, M. (2000) Individual differences in infant skills as predictors of child–caregiver joint attention and language, *Social Development*, 9: 302–15.

Matthews, J. (1999) *The Art of Childhood and Adolescence*. London: Falmer Press.

Maynard, T. and Chicken, S. (2010) Through a different lens: exploring Reggio Emilia in a Welsh context, *Early Years*, 20(1): 29–39.

McNamee, A., Mercurio, M. and Peloso, J.M. (2007) Who cares about caring in early childhood teacher education programs?, *Journal of Early Childhood Teacher Education*, 28: 277–88.

Meadows, S. and Cashdan, A. (1988) *Helping Children Learn*. London: David Fulton.

Mezirow, J. (1991) *Transformative Dimensions of Adult Learning*. San Francisco, CA: Jossey-Bass.

Miller, L. and Pound, L. (2011) Taking a critical perspective, in L. Miller and L. Pound, *Theories and Approaches to Learning in the Early Years*. London: Sage.

Mitchell, J. and Marland, P. (1989) Research on teacher thinking: the next phase, *Teaching and Teacher Education*, 5(2): 115–28.

Montie, J.E., Ziang, X. and Schweinhart, L.J. (eds) (2007) *The Role of Preschool Experience in Children's Development: Longitudinal Findings from 10 Countries*. Ypsilanti, MI: High/Scope Press.

Morgan, J. (2010) Frameworks for understanding development, in R. Parker-Rees, C. Lesson, J. Willan and J. Savage (eds) *Early Childhood Studies*. Exeter: Learning Matters.

Moss, P. (2008) Foreword, in A. Paige-Smith and A. Craft (eds) *Developing Reflective Practice in the Early Years*. Maidenhead: Open University Press.

Murray, L. (1992) The impact of postnatal depression on infant development, *Journal of Child Psychology and Psychiatry*, 33: 543–61.

Music, G. (2010) *Nurturing Natures*. London: Psychology Press.

National Association for the Education of Young Children (NAEYC) (2008) *Developmentally Appropriate Practice in Early Childhood Programs Serving Children from Birth through Age 8: A Position Statement of the National Association for the Education of Young Children.* Washington, DC: NAEYC.

National Scientific Council on the Developing Child (NSCDC) (2007) *The Timing and Quality of Early Experiences Combine to Shape Brain Architecture.* Cambridge, MA: NSCDC.

Newman, F. and Holzman, L. (1993) *Lev Vygotsky: Revolutionary Scientist.* London: Routledge.

Newson, J. and Newson, E. (1975) Intersubjectivity and the transmission of culture: on the social origins of symbolic functioning, *Bulletin of the British Psychological Society,* 28: 437–46.

New Zealand Ministry of Education (1996) *Te Whāriki: Early Childhood Curriculum.* Wellington: Learning Media.

Nias, J. (1993) Primary teachers talking: a reflexive account of longitudinal research, in M. Hammersely (ed.) *Educational Research: Current Issues.* London: Paul Chapman.

Noddings, N. (1984) *Caring.* Berkeley, CA: University of California Press.

Noddings, N. (1992) *The Challenge to Care in Schools.* New York: Teachers College Press.

Noffke, S.E. (1995) Action research and democratic schooling: problematic and potential, in S.E. Noffke and R.B. Stevenson (eds) *Educational Action Research.* New York: Teachers College Press.

O'Hanlon, C. (1993) The importance of an articulated personal theory of professional development, in J. Elliott (ed.) *Reconstructing Teacher Education.* London: Falmer Press.

Oja, S.N. and Pine, G.J. (1987) Collaborative action research: teachers' stages of development and school contexts, *Peabody Journal of Education,* 64(2): 96–115.

Olson, D.R. and Bruner, J.S. (1996) Folk psychology and folk pedagogy, in D.R. Olson and N. Torrance (eds) *The Handbook of Education and Human Development.* London: Blackwell.

Organization for Economic Cooperation and Development (OECD) (2004) *Starting Strong: Curricula and Pedagogies in Early Childhood Education and Care.* Paris: OECD Publishing.

Organization for Economic Cooperation and Development (OECD) (2009) *Doing Better for Children.* Paris: OECD Publishing.

Orme, G. (2001) *Emotionally Intelligent Living.* Carmarthen: Crown House Publishing.

Palaiologou, I. (2008) *Childhood Observation.* Exeter: Learning Matters.

Papatheodorou, T. and Moyles, J. (eds) (2009) *Learning Together in the Early Years: Exploring Relational Pedagogy.* London: Routledge.

Parker-Rees, R. (2010) Developing communication: enjoying the company of others, in R. Parker-Rees, C. Lesson, J. Willan and J. Savage (eds) *Early Childhood Studies.* Exeter: Learning Matters.

Payler, J. (2009) Co-construction and scaffolding: guidance strategies and children's meaning-making, in T. Papatheodorou and J. Moyles (eds) *Learning Together in the Early Years: Exploring Relational Pedagogy*. London: Routledge.

Pearson, E. and Degotardi, S. (2009) Education for sustainable development in early childhood education: a global solution to local concerns?, *International Journal of Early Childhood*, 41(2): 97–111.

Perry, W.G. (1981) Cognitive and ethical growth: the making of meaning, in A.W. Chickering and Associates (eds) *The Modern American College*. San Francisco, CA: Jossey-Bass.

Piaget, J. (1970) *The Science of Education and the Psychology of the Child*. New York: Grossman.

Piaget, J. (1978) *The Development of Thought*. Oxford: Blackwell.

Pine, J. (1994) The language of primary caregivers, in C. Gallaway and B. Richards (eds) *Input and Interaction in Language Acquisition*. Cambridge: Cambridge University Press.

Pramling Samuelsson, I. and Kaga, Y. (eds) (2008) *The Contribution of Early Childhood Education to a Sustainable Society*. Paris: UNESCO.

QCDA, (2010) *Assessment and Reporting Arrangements: CYPS and KSI*. Coventry: Qualifications and Curriculum Development Agency.

Quortrup, J. (1987) Introduction: the sociology of childhood, *International Journal of Sociology*, 17(3): 3–37.

Rinaldi, C. (2005a) *In Dialogue with Reggio Emilia*. London: Routledge.

Rinaldi, C. (2005b) Documentation and assessment: what is the relationship?, in A. Clark, A.T. Kjorholt and P. Moss (eds) *Beyond Listening: Children's Perspectives on Early Childhood Services*. Bristol: Policy Press.

Roberts, C. and Roberts, J. (2007) Greener by degrees, in C. Roberts and J. Roberts (eds) *Greener by Degrees: Exploring Sustainability through Higher Education Curricula*. Cheltenham: Centre for Active Learning, University of Gloucestershire.

Roberts, R. (2002) *Self-esteem and Early Learning*. London: Paul Chapman.

Rogers, C. (1967) The interpersonal relationship in the facilitation of learning. Reprinted in H. Kirschenbaum and V. L. Henderson (eds) (1990) *The Carl Rogers Reader*. London: Constable.

Rogers, S. (2007) Creative teaching, in J. Willan, R. Parker-Rees and J. Savage (eds) *Early Childhood Studies*. Exeter: Learning Matters.

Rogers, S. (2010) Powerful pedagogies and playful resistance: researching children's perspectives, in E. Brooker and S. Edwards (eds) *Engaging Play*. Maidenhead: Open University Press.

Rogers, S. and Evans, J. (2008) *Inside Role-Play in Early Education*. London: Routledge.

Rogers, S. and Rose, J. (2007) Ready for reception? The advantages and disadvantages of single-point entry to school, *Early Years*, 27(1): 47–63.

Rogoff, B. (1990) *Apprenticeships in Thinking*. New York: Oxford University Press.

Rogoff, B., Turkanis, C.G. and Bartlett, L. (eds) (2001) *Learning Together: Children and Adults in a School Community*. New York: Oxford University Press.

Rose, J. (2001) The impact of action research on practitioners' thinking: a supporting case for action research as a method of professional development. Unpublished PhD thesis, Goldsmiths College, University of London.

Rose, J. (2006) *The Independent Review of the Teaching of Early Reading*. Nottingham: DfES.

Salovey, P. and Mayer, J.D. (1990) Emotional intelligence, *Imagination, Cognition and Personality*, 9: 185–211.

Schaffer, H. and Emerson, P. (1964) The development of social attachments in infancy, *Monographs of the Society for Research in Child Development*, 29(3): Serial 94.

Schön, D. (1987) *Educating the Reflective Practitioner*. San Francisco, CA: Jossey-Bass.

Schweinhart, L.J., Barnes, H.V. and Weikart, D.P. (1993) Significant benefits: the High/Scope Perry Preschool Study through age 27, *Monographs of the High/Scope Educational Research Foundation, 10*. Ypsilanti, MI: High/Scope Press.

Seligman, M.E.P., Reivich, K., Jaycock, L. and Gilhamm, J. (1995) *The Optimistic Child*. New York: Harper Perennial.

Shavelson, R.J. and Stern, P. (1981) Research on teachers' pedagogical thoughts, judgements, decisions and behavior, *Review of Educational Research*, 51(4): 455–98.

Shier, H. (2001) Pathways to participation: openings, opportunities and obligations, *Children and Society*, 15(2): 107–17.

Shor, I. (1992) *Empowering Education: Critical Teaching for Social Change*. Chicago, IL: University of Chicago Press.

Siegel, D.J. (1999) *The Developing Mind: Toward a Neurobiology of Interpersonal Experience*. New York: Guilford Press.

Siraj-Blatchford, I. (1994) *The Early Years: Laying the Foundations for Racial Equality*. Stoke-on-Trent: Trentham Books.

Siraj-Blatchford, I. (2007) Diversity, inclusion and learning in the early years, in J. Moyles (ed.) *Early Years Foundations: Meeting the Challenge*. Maidenhead: Open University Press.

Siraj-Blatchford, I. and Manni, L. (2008) 'Would you like to tidy up now?' An analysis of adult questioning in the English Foundation Stage, *Early Years*, 28(1): 5–22.

Siraj-Blatchford, I., Sylva, K., Mattock, S., Gilden, R. and Bell, D. (2002) *Researching Effective Pedagogy in the Early Years (REPEY)*. London: HMSO.

Smilansky, S. and Shefatya, L. (1990) *Facilitating Play*. Silver Spring, MD: Psychological and Educational Publications.

Smith, F. (2004) *Understanding Reading*. Hillsdale, NJ: Erlbaum.

Smith, P.K. (2010) *Children and their Play*. Oxford: Blackwell.

Smith, P.K., Cowie, H. and Blades, M. (2004) *Understanding Children's Development*. London: Blackwell.

Sroufe, A. (1995) *Emotional Development*. Cambridge: Cambridge University Press.

Sutton-Smith, B. (1971) The role of play in cognitive development, in R. Herron and B. Sutton-Smith (eds) *Child's Play*. New York: Wiley.

Swick, K.J. (2007) Insights on caring for early childhood professionals and families, *Early Childhood Education Journal*, 35(2): 97–102.

Sylva, K., Melhuish, E., Sammons, P., Siraj-Blatchford, I. and Taggart, C. (2010) *Early Childhood Matters: Evidence from the Effective Preschool and Primary Education Project*. London: Routledge.

Taggart, G. (2011) Don't we care? The ethics of emotional labour of early years professionalism, *Early Years*, 31(1): 85–95.

Thomas, A. and Chess, S. (1977) *Temperament and Development*. New York: Brunnel/ Mazel.

Thomas, S. (2008) *Nurturing Babies and Children Under Four*. London: Pearson.

Thompson, R.A. (1990) On emotion and self-regulation, in R.A. Thompson (ed.) *Nebraska Symposium on Motivation*, 36: 383–483. Lincoln, NB: University of Nebraska Press.

Tickell, C. (2010) *The Early Years: Foundations for Life, Health and Learning* [online]. Available at: http://www.education.gov.uk/tickellreview [accessed 12 September 2011].

Torff, B. (1999) Tacit knowledge in teaching: folk pedagogy and teacher education, in R.J. Sternberg and J.A. Hovarth (eds) *Tacit Knowledge in Professional Practice*. London: Erlbaum.

Tovey, H. (2010) Playing on the edge: perceptions of risk and danger in outdoor play, in P. Broadhead, J. Howard and E. Wood (eds) *Play and Learning in the Early Years*. London: Sage.

Trevarthan, C. (1993) Playing into reality: conversations with the infant communi- cator, *Winnicott Studies*, 7(Spring): 67–84.

Trevarthan, C. and Aitken, K.J. (2001) Infant intersubjectivity, research, theory, and clinical applications, *Journal of Child Psychological Psychiatry*, 42(1): 3–48.

Tzuo, P.W. (2007) The tension between teacher control and children's freedom in a child-centred classroom: resolving the practical dilemma through a close look at the related theories, *Early Childhood Education Journal*, 35(1): 33–9.

Underdown, A. (2007) *Young Children's Health and Well-being*. Maidenhead: Open University Press.

UNICEF (2001) *The State of the World's Children*. New York: UNICEF.

Unrau, N.J. (1997) *Thoughtful Teachers, Thoughtful Learners*. Scarborough, ONT: Pippin.

Vygtosky, L. (1978) *Mind in Society: The Development of Higher Psychological Processes*. Cambridge, MA: Harvard University Press.

Vygotsky, L. (1986) *Thought and Language* (revised and edited by A. Kozulin). Cambridge, MA: MIT Press.

Waite, S., Evans, J. and Rogers, S. (2011) A time of change: outdoor learning and pedagogies of transition between foundation stage and year 1, in S. Waite (ed.) *Children Learning Outside the Classroom*, London: Sage.

Walsh, D. (2005) Developmental theory and early childhood education: necessary but not sufficient, in N. Yelland (ed.) *Critical Issues in Early Childhood Education.* Maidenhead: Open University Press.

Warming, H. (2005) Participant observation: a way to learn about children's perspectives, in A. Clark, A.T. Kjorholt, A.T. and P. Moss (eds) *Beyond Listening: Children's Perspectives on Early Childhood Services.* Bristol: Policy Press.

Wenger, E. (1998) *Communities of Practice: Learning, Meaning and Identity.* Cambridge: Cambridge University Press.

Whitehead, M. (2002) *Developing Language and Literacy with Young Children.* London: Paul Chapman.

Whitehead, M. (2007) 'Hi granny! I'm writing a novel'. Literacy in early childhood: joys, issues and challenges, in J. Moyles (ed.) *Early Years Foundations: Meeting the Challenges.* Maidenhead: Open University Press.

Willan, J. (2010) Observing children, in R. Parker-Rees, C. Leeson, J. Willan and J. Savage (eds) *Early Childhood Studies.* Exeter: Learning Matters.

Wolfendale, S. (1997) *Meeting Special Needs in the Early Years.* London: David Fulton.

Wood, D. (1998) *How Children Think and Learn: The Social Contexts of Cognitive Development.* Oxford: Blackwell.

Wood, E. (2007) Reconceptualising child-centred education: contemporary directions in policy, theory and practice in early childhood, *Forum,* 49(1/2): 119–33.

Worthington, M. (2007) Multi-modality, play and children's mark-making in maths, in J. Moyles (ed.) *Early Years Foundations: Meeting the Challenges.* Maidenhead: Open University Press.

Yinger, R. and Hendricks-Lee, M. (1993) Working knowledge in teaching, in C. Day, J. Calderhead and P. Denicolo (eds) *Research on Teaching Thinking.* London: Falmer Press.

Zeichner, K.M. (1993) Connecting genuine teacher development to the struggle for social justice, *Journal of Education for Teaching,* 19(1): 5–20.

Index

STARTING FROM THE CHILD
Third Edition

Julie Fisher

9780335223848 (Paperback)
2007

eBook also available

In a practical and realistic way, the third edition of *Starting from the Child* supports practitioners in the Foundation Stage to be advocates for young children and their learning needs. Julie Fisher outlines the important theories and research which should underpin decisions about best practice. She offers meaningful and inspirational ways of developing appropriate learning environments and experiences for Foundation Stage children.

Key features:

- An extended explanation of how to plan for child-initiated learning alongside adult-initiated learning
- A completely revised chapter on 'The place of play', with a new focus on different types and contexts for play, cultural influences and the role of the adult in supporting play
- Two new chapters on the observation and assessment of children's learning, and self-evaluation for practitioners

www.openup.co.uk

 OPEN UNIVERSITY PRESS
McGraw - Hill Education

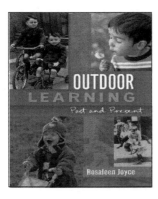

OUTDOOR LEARNING
Past and Present

Rosaleen Joyce

9780335243013 (Paperback)
January 2012

eBook also available

The book breaks new ground by placing 'outdoor learning' in a
theoretical, historical and social context of changing understandings of
children, childhood and the use of the outdoors. The books approach
is based on the premise that ideas phase in and out of use depending
on social and political contexts. This perspective will help people to
think about how present day attitudes regarding outdoor learning
came to be, where they came from and to question their 'newness'.

Key features:

- Provides a reflective approach to practice
- Effective training for practitioners in their use of the outdoors -
  recognising the different approaches required from those used in
  the indoor classroom
- Places outdoor learning in an historical, social and political
  context, exploring our changing understandings of children,
  childhood and the use of the outdoors

www.openup.co.uk

PARENTS AND PROFESSIONALS IN EARLY CHILDHOOD SETTINGS

Glenda MacNaughton
and Patrick Hughes

9780335243730 (Paperback)
2011

eBook also available

Parents and Professionals in Early Childhood Settings addresses the complex and sometimes controversial issues that emerge from the care and education of young children. Staff and parents in early childhood settings can find ample advice about how to promote good communication, but much of that advice has no grounding in their daily lives. Instead, it prescribes an established set menu of communication tools, such as newsletters, notebooks and message boards that rarely respond to what staff and families say about relationships between them.

Key features:

- Covers a range of 'issue stories' which the reader can dip into as appropriate and which draw on research into relationships between staff and families
- Each chapter or story will feature the voices and perspectives of 'real staff' and families, illustrating the complex, difficult and/or controversial issue and highlighting the questions of power and knowledge that emerge
- Fairness Alerts to help the reader see, understand and break unfair thinking habits

www.openup.co.uk

RECONCEPTUALIZING LEADERSHIP IN THE EARLY YEARS

Rory McDowall Clark and Janet Murray

9780335246243 (Paperback)
August 2012

eBook also available

This book explores the realities of leadership in the early years and examines the challenges and opportunities for the profession. The authors suggest that recent moves to professionalize the workforce offer a unique opportunity to reconceptualize leadership and develop a new paradigm more suited to the specific circumstances of the sector.

Key features:

- Ideas based on research from a wide range of current early years practice
- Real leadership profiles of practitioners from a diversity of different professional backgrounds and working in a variety of contexts
- Reflective prompts to assist you in identifying the leadership in your own practice and how this can be developed further

www.openup.co.uk

OBSERVATION
Origins and Approaches in
Early Childhood

Valerie Podmore and Paulette Luff

9780335244249 (Paperback)
2012

eBook also available

"This book is an excellent resource for all those studying or working in the field of early childhood. It deals with key issues of observational processes offering a balance between theory and practical activities. It is written in a critical, engaging and informative way, with scope for interesting discussions with students, and is a useful tool for lecturers and students as in learning about observations for all involved in early childhood education."
Dr. Ioanna Palaiologou, Lecturer, University of Hull, UK

Key features:

- An adaptation of a book that has been successful in New Zealand – updated with UK content
- Rich in examples, drawing on a variety of studies, policies and contexts to illustrate key points
- A range of practical techniques, both qualitative and quantitative for practitioners

www.openup.co.uk

OPEN UNIVERSITY PRESS
McGraw - Hill Education

**SAFEGUARDING BABIES AND
YOUNG CHILDREN
A Guide for Early Years
Professionals**

John Powell and Elaine Uppal

9780335234080 (Paperback)
2012

eBook also available

This practical and challenging book focuses on the relationship that
early years professionals have with babies, young children and their
families/carers. Powell and Uppal reprioritize practice in safeguarding
and child protection, and emphasizing the importance of focusing on
the skills needed to work successfully in this arena.

Key features:

- Highly practical discussion about safeguarding babies and young
  children
- A brief history and overview of a number of issues and their
  relevance for practice
- Case studies allowing the reader to rehearse their possible
  approaches to a particular scenario

www.openup.co.uk

 OPEN UNIVERSITY PRESS
McGraw - Hill Education

MAKING SENSE OF THEORY & PRACTICE IN EARLY CHILDHOOD
The Power of Ideas

Tim Waller, Judy Whitmarsh
and Karen Clarke (Eds)

9780335242467 (Paperback)
2011

eBook also available

This accessible book demystifies the links between theory and practice for those studying in the field of early childhood. The book encourages those new to research to develop their investigations as straightforward narrative accounts of the phenomenon that they are investigating.

Throughout the book the authors demonstrate the influence of theoretical perspectives on their own practice and research. They articulate how this adds depth to their studies by linking into wider and more enduring themes.

Key features:

- Theoretical concepts, which are related to practice and/or research
- Case studies
- Examples from research practice enabling readers to explore the practical application of the 'big ideas'

www.openup.co.uk

OPEN UNIVERSITY PRESS
McGraw - Hill Education